ID0786386

Wales

Wales

BY LIZ SONNEBORN

Enchantment of the World™
Second Series

CHILDREN'S PRESS®

An Imprint of Scholastic Inc.

Frontispiece: **Houses in Tenby, Pembrokeshire**

Consultant: Robert Austin, PhD, Associate Professor, Centre for European, Russian and Eurasian Studies, University of Toronto, Toronto, Ontario

Please note: All statistics are as up-to-date as possible at the time of publication.

Book production by The Design Lab

Library of Congress Cataloging-in-Publication Data
Names: Sonneborn, Liz, author.
Title: Wales / by Liz Sonneborn.
Description: New York, NY : Children's Press, an Imprint of Scholastic, 2018.
  | Series: Enchantment of the world | Includes bibliographical references
  and index.
Identifiers: LCCN 2017028548 | ISBN 9780531235928 (library binding)
Subjects: LCSH: Wales—Juvenile literature.
Classification: LCC DA708 .S66 2018 | DDC 942.9—dc23
LC record available at https://lccn.loc.gov/2017028548

Scholastic Inc., 557 Broadway, New York, NY 10012

1 2 3 4 5 6 7 8 9 10 R 27 26 25 24 23 22 21 20 19 18

Welsh pony

Contents

Left to right: **Gower Peninsula, Brecon Beacons National Park, puffins, Tintern Abbey, sheep**

CHAPTER 1

The Prince of Wales

O N September 16, 1400, Owain Glyndwr gathered friends and family at his estate. Before the crowd, he made an outrageous, even dangerous declaration. Glyndwr named himself the true Prince of Wales.

The country of Wales is located on the western side of the island of Great Britain in Europe. Directly to the east of Wales lies England. When Glyndwr made his declaration, Wales had been controlled by England for more than a hundred years. After the English took control, the title of Prince of Wales no longer belonged to the Welsh, the people of Wales. It was now bestowed on the eldest son of the king of England.

By announcing that he was the Prince of Wales, Glyndwr was openly defying the English king. He was also lighting the spark that would inflame a rebellion.

Opposite: **Owain Glyndwr led thousands of men in his revolt against the English.**

Defying the King

Born in about 1350, Glyndwr came from a distinguished Welsh family that lived near the English border. He was comfortable in English society. Glyndwr had spent time in the English capital of London. He had also served in the king's army.

So why did Glyndwr suddenly decide to challenge the

king? He may have been angry because the king had not made him a knight and given him the privileges that came with that honor. Glyndwr may have been upset that the king did not come to his aid in a dispute with an English landowner. Or he may have just seen that the time was right to seize power.

The land in Wales is a mix of rocky mountains and rolling hills.

Dreams of a Free Wales

Glyndwr knew that the Welsh people were unhappy being under England's thumb. The Welsh were desperately poor and felt exploited by the English. The English looked down on them and restricted their rights. The Welsh felt like second-class citizens in their own country.

Many old Welsh stories told of princes who had ruled Wales long ago. Glyndwr imagined himself as a leader in their mold. As Prince of Wales, he believed he could rally his beleaguered people and restore his nation to its former glory.

Conwy Castle was built between 1283 and 1289. It is considered one of the finest fortresses in Europe.

Clever and charismatic, Glyndwr amassed a small army. His men began attacking English towns in northeast Wales. But the rebellion's greatest early success came on April 1, 1401. Two cousins of Glyndwr's led a force of forty men in taking over Conwy Castle.

The attack had great symbolic meaning to the Welsh. The English had built castles all over Wales. The soldiers stationed there were charged with keeping the Welsh in line. Taking over one of the grandest castles with so few men impressed the Welsh. They began to think that perhaps somehow Glyndwr's rebellion might actually succeed.

Glyndwr's men mostly staged quick raids and surprise attacks. But on June 22, 1402, they met the English army in a full-fledged battle. To the shock of everyone, Glyndwr's ragged troops managed to defeat the professional English force.

Word of the great victory spread. More and more Welshmen joined the fight. By the summer of 1403, Glyndwr's forces had gained a hold over nearly every region in Wales.

A Welsh Hero

Glyndwr's army had some amazing victories, but it was no match for the English forces in the long run. Low on supplies and weapons, the tide started turning against Glyndwr and the Welsh army. The English took back Wales, bit by bit. By 1408, the Welsh had lost control of every part of the country.

In 1404, Owain Glyndwr formed a parliament, a law-making body. Creating a Welsh parliament was an important step toward creating an independent Wales.

Many of Glyndwr's supporters were killed, but he managed to escape.

Pockets of resistance continued to fight the English, but the rebellion slowly petered out. The Welsh resigned themselves once again to English rule, yet they remained true to Glyndwr.

Glyndwr lived out his life as a fugitive, hiding in caves and forests. No Welsh person, however, gave him up to the authorities. In 1415, one chronicler wrote, "Many say that he died, but the prophets say that he did not die."

Welsh people relax at a café in Cardiff. Many people in Wales identify themselves as Welsh rather than as both Welsh and British.

And these prophets were in a sense correct. Glyndwr the man might have died, but his legend lives on. In fact, the people of Wales now celebrate him as a national hero.

Revering Glyndwr

In the six hundred years since Glyndwr's rebellion, Wales has not won the independence it dreamed of. It is part of the United Kingdom, a country made up of Wales, England, Scotland, and Northern Ireland. In some ways, Wales is also still under England's shadow. Throughout their history, the Welsh have often felt resentment toward the English. Even though they share a country, the Welsh sometimes complain that the English do not respect them or take their concerns seriously.

United Kingdom

Glyndwr may have failed in his mission to create a free Wales, but the Welsh still hold him in high regard because he embodied so many of the qualities they revere. He was a bold and fearless leader, unwilling to back down no matter what. He was an underdog who, with grit and determination, dared to defy wealthy and powerful enemies. And most of all, he was a proud Welshman who was willing to fight and die for his land and his people.

CHAPTER 2

Land of Cliffs and Castles

LOOK AROUND IN WALES AND YOU WILL SEE beautiful landscapes. The nation has high mountains, lush woods, spectacular waterfalls, and golden beaches. Perhaps Wales is best known for its rough and rugged coastline, where crystal blue waves dash into the sides of rocky cliffs.

Opposite: **A narrow strip of land juts into the sea near Swansea, in southern Wales.**

Geographic Features of Wales

Area: 8,015 square miles (20,759 sq km)

Highest Elevation: Mount Snowdon, 3,556 feet (1,084 m)

Length of Border with England: 160 miles (257 km)

Largest Island: Anglesey, 261 square miles (676 sq km)

Longest River: Severn, 220 miles (354 km)

Largest Lake: Bala Lake, 1.9 square miles (4.9 sq km)

Largest Reservoir: Lake Vyrnwy, 1.7 square miles (4.4 sq km)

Largest National Park: Snowdonia National Park, 838 square miles (2,170 sq km)

Average Daily High Temperature: In Cardiff, 47°F (8°C) in January, 71°F (22°C) in July

Average Daily Low Temperature: In Cardiff, 36°F (2°C) in January, 56°F (13°C) in July

Average Annual Precipitation: 50 inches (127 cm)

Where in the World Is Wales?

Wales is a small country located in western Europe, on the western edge of the island of Great Britain. Great Britain also includes Scotland and England. Wales's only land border is with England, which is situated directly to the east.

The rest of Wales is bound by water. To the north is the Irish Sea, which lies between Wales and the island of Ireland. To the west is Cardigan Bay and St. George's Channel. And to the south is the Bristol Channel.

Several islands are considered part of Wales. Anglesey is the largest. Located just off the northwest coast, it is separated from the mainland by the Menai Strait. Today, Anglesey and the mainland are linked by two bridges.

Many lighthouses were built along the Welsh coast to warn ships of the rocky land.

Offa's Dyke

In the late eighth century, Offa was the Saxon king of Mercia, located in what is now western England. He was wary of the rowdy rival rulers to the west in present-day Wales. To protect his land, he ordered an ambitious building project. He had his subjects build a wall of earth that marked the boundary between his realm and neighboring Welsh kingdoms. The long border wall became known as Offa's Dyke.

In many places, Offa's Dyke runs along the present-day border of Wales and England. The Welsh still sometimes refer to England using the phrase "beyond Offa's Dyke." The ancient earthwork is preserved today as the Offa's Dyke Path. On this national trail, hikers can take in some of the most beautiful scenery of both countries.

Spreading over 8,015 square miles (20,759 square kilometers), Wales is a little smaller than the state of New Jersey. Wales is the second-smallest nation in the United Kingdom, after Northern Ireland. Scotland is more than three times larger than Wales; England, more than five times larger. Wales includes just over 9 percent the United Kingdom's total land base.

Mountains, Rivers, and Lakes

Much of Wales is covered by hills and mountains. The Cambrian Mountains run like a backbone down the nation's center. The highest peaks of the Cambrian range are found in the Snowdonia area to the northwest. The tallest mountain in Wales is the rugged and rocky Mount Snowdon, which rises to the height of 3,556 feet (1,084 meters). It is the third-highest mountain in the United Kingdom.

Lowlands are mostly found on the island of Anglesey and in the region near the English border. There are also sandy beaches in the north and west of Wales. Resorts there attract tourists from England and the rest of Europe who come to enjoy the sand and scenery. Much of the coastline is also marked by soaring cliffs.

Low-lying areas also include the bottom of deep river valleys. The rivers of Wales include the Dee in the north, the Clwyd in the northeast, and Rheidol in the west. The nation's two longest rivers are found in the southeast. The Severn

Towering cliffs rise from the sea in Pembrokeshire.

measures 220 miles (354 km); the Wye, 134 miles (216 km). Both the Severn and the Wye flow into England and empty into the Bristol Channel.

Wales is dotted with small lakes. The largest natural body of water is Bala Lake, located in eastern Snowdonia. Wales also has several manmade reservoirs that trap water that flows down the mountains. The reservoirs provide water for English cities, such as Liverpool and Birmingham.

A Mild Climate

The mountains of Wales block cold winds from the east. As a result, its weather tends to be mild and pleasant. In Cardiff, Wales's capital, the average high temperature is 71 degrees Fahrenheit (22 degrees Celsius) in July and 47°F (8°C) in January. Temperatures vary somewhat in other regions. Generally, coastal areas are the warmest, and mountainous areas are the coolest.

Cities in Wales

For much of its history, Wales was a rural country. Most people lived on small farms and in villages scattered throughout the countryside. Since the mid-seventeenth century, though, a few cities emerged with the development of the iron and coal industries. Like the Welsh capital of Cardiff, with a population of about 346,000, they are mostly clustered in southern Wales.

Home to about 182,000, Swansea (below) is Wales's second-largest city. It is located only about 35 miles (56 km) northwest of Cardiff. Sitting on the shore of Bristol Bay, Swansea is known for its lively waterfront. A leading attraction in Swansea is the Dylan Thomas Centre, which honors Wales's most famous poet.

With about 130,000 residents, the city of Newport (right) lies to Cardiff's northeast. It is a manufacturing center that produces chemicals, aluminum, and paper. Newport's Riverfront Arts Centre has showcased a

variety of music, dance, drama, and comedy performances since opening in 2004. On the outskirts of the city is Tredegar House. The mansion, built in the 1600s, was the home of a noble Welsh family. The house and nearby gardens are now open to the public.

Merthyr Tydfil was named for St. Tydfil, who died there in the fifth century. The city was once an important center for the iron and coal industries. The mines have closed, but Merthyr Tydfil remains a vibrant city with a population of approximately 44,000. In addition to enjoying the city's scenic nature trails, residents and visitors can take a vintage steam train into nearby Brecon Beacons, one of Wales's three national parks.

A woman stands behind one of the many waterfalls at Brecon Beacons National Park.

Rainy days are not uncommon in Wales. Overall, the nation sees an average of about 50 inches (127 centimeters) of rain annually. The southern portion of Wales is the driest region. Winds blowing off the Atlantic Ocean often bring rain to the mountains in the north. This region might get 100 inches (254 cm) of precipitation. In higher elevations, snow falls about ten days a year.

Preserving Wales's Natural Beauty

The Welsh people are justifiably proud of their country's natural beauty and are eager to see its lands preserved and protected. Almost 20 percent of Wales is designated as national parklands. Of the United Kingdom's fifteen national parks, three are located in Wales. These parks include many towns and villages. More than eighty thousand Welsh people are lucky enough to live amid the gorgeous scenery of a national park.

The largest park is Snowdonia National Park in the northwest. It features hiking paths, bike trails, and a railway that takes visitors to the summit of Mount Snowdon. In southeastern Wales, the Brecon Beacons National Park is known for its picturesque caves, gorges, and waterfalls. The Pembrokeshire Coast National Park in the southwest is celebrated as one of the greatest coastal parks in the world. Its attractions include its sandy beaches, secluded coves, and rugged cliffs.

The British government also recognizes five places in Wales as Areas of Outstanding Natural Beauty: the Anglesey coast, the Gower Peninsula, the Llyn Peninsula, the Wye Valley, and the Clwydian mountain range and Dee Valley. The natural landscapes and wildlife in these areas are protected by law from destruction or development.

A hiker enjoys the view from atop a ledge in Snowdonia National Park. More than four million people visit the park every year.

CHAPTER 3

Living Things

THE COUNTRYSIDE OF WALES IS RICH IN PLANT AND animal life. Its forests, grasslands, mountains, and shores are ideal habitats for a wide range of living things.

More than one thousand types of plants grow in Wales. A few of them are found nowhere else. For instance, Ley's whitebeam is a tree found only on two limestone cliffs in the Brecon Beacons, making it Wales's rarest tree. There are now about sixteen Ley's whitebeams alive in the wild.

Opposite: **Heather covers a stretch of land along the coast in southern Wales. A hardy plant that can thrive in poor soil, heather is the dominant plant in open areas of Wales.**

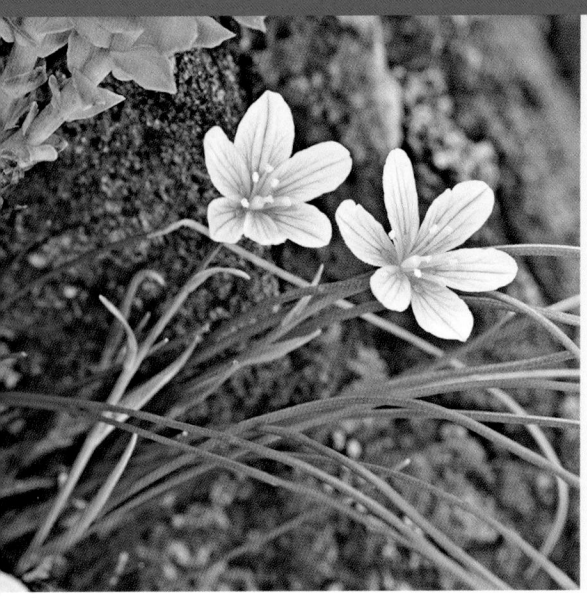

The Snowdon Lily

For more than ten thousand years, the Snowdon lily has grown in Snowdonia in northwest Wales. This plant thrives on the cold mountain slopes in the region. Technically, it is a spiderwort plant, not a lily. It got its named from the lilylike white flowers that it sprouts in early summer. The rest of the year, the plant looks like shoots of grass.

The Snowdon lily now faces dual threats. As the earth's temperatures warm, the plant may soon not be able to survive in its natural habitat. Conservationists also worry about careless mountain climbers stomping on the plants that remain in wilderness areas.

Forests and Grasslands

Several thousand years ago, much of Wales was covered with forests. Native trees included birches, oaks, junipers, and elms. Over time, though, the forests were cleared to make way first for grazing lands for animals and later for mines and industry.

Today, woodlands make up only about 14 percent of Wales. Most of these forests were recently planted with Sitka spruce, a non-native tree. The largest woodland area with trees native to Wales is the Pengelli Forest. Located in western Wales, it has been filled with oak trees since ancient times.

Grass covers much of the countryside where forests once stood. These grasslands are full of colorful wildflowers such as cowslips, bluebells, and orchids. Other flowering plants of Wales include the butterwort, which grows in the wet grasslands of the southwest. It consumes insects it traps with its sticky leaves. The mountainous region of Snowdonia is adorned with purple saxifrage. This plant's tight clusters of flowers add a dash of color to the chilly rock faces there.

The Daffodil and the Leek

Every March 1, the Welsh celebrate St. David's Day, which honors the patron saint of Wales. Many people mark the day by pinning a daffodil to their lapel. These bright yellow flowers bloom each spring just in time for the St. David's Day festivities. In recent times, the daffodil has become a beloved symbol of Wales.

But another plant—the leek—has an even longer association with the Welsh people. The bulb of the leek is a vegetable with an onion-like bite often used in Welsh cooking. Legend holds that, in the sixth century, St. David told a group of Welsh soldiers preparing to fight the Saxons to wear a leek on their clothing. In the heat of battle, the leeks would help them tell their fellow Welsh from their enemies.

Although the story might not be true, some people choose to wear a leek to celebrate St. David's Day. Traditionally, Welsh soldiers also honor the saint each year by eating an entire leek raw.

Beasts, Large and Small

Of all the animals of Wales, the one most important to its economy is the sheep. Wales's grasslands are ideal grazing grounds. The sheep population has exploded in recent years. It is now almost ten million—more than three sheep for every person!

In addition to sheep, many farmers in Wales also raise cattle. The country is particularly well known for one breed—the Welsh black. The only cattle breed native to Wales, these black-furred animals have distinctive white horns with black tips. Their tasty meat and milk are prized by chefs.

Several other large mammals live wild in the Welsh

The Ponies of the Carneddau

The wild ponies of the Carneddau Mountains are survivors. Some five hundred years ago, King Henry VIII called for them all to be slaughtered. They were useless, he declared, because they were too small for his knights to ride.

The ponies, though, managed to save themselves from the king's cruel order. Able to run on rocky terrain, many successfully hid from their executioners. The tough animals also weathered a brutal winter in 2013. Some died standing up, frozen to death. But because of their hardy constitution, most made it through.

Now the ponies are protected by the government of Wales. They are permitted to roam freely through Snowdonia most of the time. Once a year, farmers and volunteers work together to round them up, and each pony gets a health checkup before being released into the wild once again.

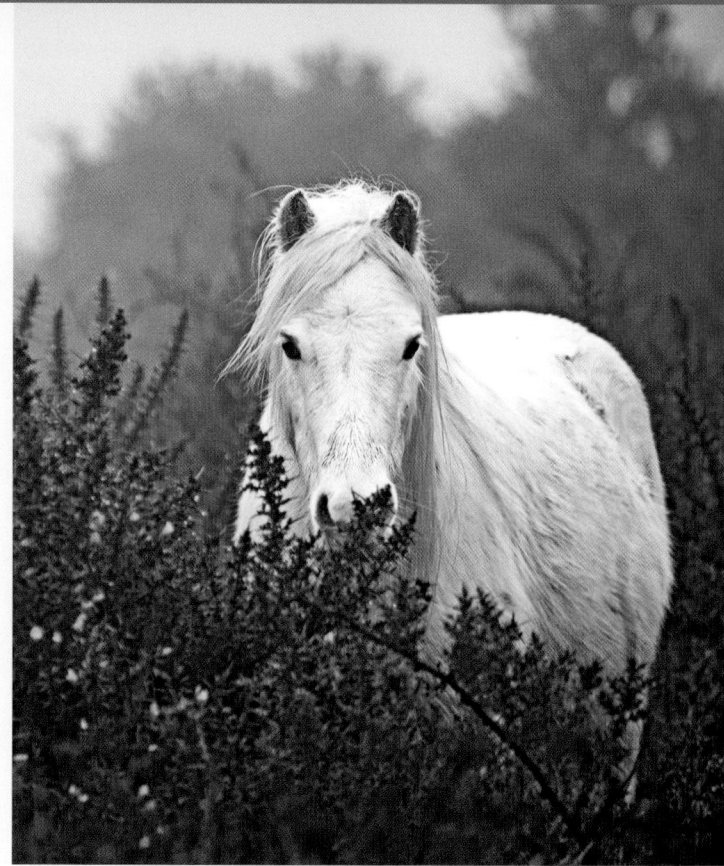

countryside. Deer and goats are particularly common in the Snowdonia region. The area is also home to a famed herd of about two hundred wild ponies.

Many other small mammals live in Wales. They include foxes, badgers, brown hares, rats, mice, and gray and red squirrels. Polecats are common in rural areas. These weasel-like animals are nocturnal. During their nighttime hunts, they feed on birds, snakes, and lizards. Known by their long fluffy tails, small numbers of pine martens make a comfortable home in the forests of Sitka pines. The tiny Skomer vole is found only in Wales. About twenty thousand live on Skomer Island, off the country's west coast.

Life in the Water

With its long coastline, Wales is also hospitable to sea mammals. About one hundred bottlenose dolphins live in Cardigan Bay off western Wales. Atlantic gray seals are found in Pembrokeshire Coast National Park and on nearby islands. The Pembrokeshire shores are a breeding ground for these seals. Every autumn, about one thousand seal pups are born there. Whale watchers also flock to the area in hopes of spying one of the fin whales or blue whales that sometimes make an appearance in coastal waters.

Across Wales, many species of fish swim off the coast or in rivers, streams, and lakes. Trout, salmon, perch, and pike are just a few examples. The rare gwyniad can be found only in Bala Lake. This species of whitefish has lived there for some ten thousand years.

Polecats often have more than one den, where they can rest safely. They come out at night to hunt rats, mice, rabbits, and other small creatures.

Coastal waters are also rich with shellfish such as oysters and mussels. The coast of the Gower Peninsula is known for the abundance of small shellfish called cockles. Fried cockles are often part of a traditional Welsh breakfast.

Reptiles, Insects, and Birds

The countryside of Wales is home to frogs, toads, newts, and lizards. Two species of snakes are native to the country—the harmless grass snake and the poisonous adder. The slow worm

People collect cockles along the Welsh shore. Cockles can be found in sandy areas at low tide.

at first glance might look like a snake, but the slithering creature is really a legless lizard.

The insects of Wales include the southern damselfly of the Pengelli Forest, the great green bush cricket of the Gower Peninsula, and the rainbow leaf beetle of Snowdonia. The holly blue butterfly is often seen in churchyards. It lays its eggs in the holly or ivy that often grows on old buildings.

Many seabirds thrive along the shores of Wales. Among them are herons, swans, geese, ducks, and cormorants. A favorite of bird-watchers is the squat puffin. These small black-and-white birds have strong wings and large beaks. Every spring, their beaks turn bright orange to help them attract mates during breeding season.

Puffins feed by diving into the sea and catching fish. They are unusual in that they can collect several fish in a single dive.

The Red Kite

The red kite of Wales has a great comeback story. A few decades ago, only a few of these majestic hawks lived in the wild. But through conservation efforts, their numbers have swelled. A red kite flying overhead is now a common sight.

True to their name, red kites have reddish-brown feathers on their bodies, forked tails, and long narrow wings. They are large birds, but they are light and graceful in the air. They soar and glide with only an occasional slight flap of their wings. The kites people make out of wood and paper are named after this species.

Red kites are scavengers that feed on dead animals, although they also sometimes eat worms and small birds. In Wales, red kites can also find a meal at the Red Kite Feeding Station in Brecon Beacons National Park. Every day, park visitors gather to watch fifty or more red kites slowly dive from the sky at feeding time.

The islands of Wales also have large populations of migrating birds, such as the gannet and the chough. Skomer Island is an important breeding ground for the Manx shearwater. These birds are known for flying low over the water, rarely beating their wings. With about 120,000 pairs arriving each year, Skomer Island has probably the largest colony of Manx shearwaters in the world.

There are also many land birds that fly above the Welsh countryside. They include owls, hawks, falcons, and red kites. The red kite has become something of an unofficial national bird of Wales. The gardens of Wales attract a host of small birds such as finches, yellowhammers, and European robins.

Protecting Welsh Wildlife

In 2013, a report by twenty-five conservation groups set off an alarm bell in Wales. It claimed that farming practices and human activity were threatening many species of plants and animals. The report concluded by calling on the Welsh government to take action before it was too late.

The Welsh government is now trying to reverse these trends. It has committed itself to protecting Wales's biodiversity—the many varied forms of life found in its natural environments. The government is working with the Wales Biodiversity Partnership to create plans that will ensure the survival of all the nation's plants and animals.

Children scramble through a moss-covered forest near the Arran River in northern Wales. The Welsh government is committed to protecting the nation's environment, for the sake of the plants and animals and so that people can enjoy it.

CHAPTER 4

Historic Wales

ABOUT 250,000 YEARS AGO, EARLY HUMANS began living in what is now Wales. The landscape was then cold, harsh, and forbidding. But about ten thousand years ago, at the end of the Ice Age, the climate warmed. The region became covered with dense forests and was much more hospitable to human and animal life.

People in Wales first lived by hunting game and gathering plants. In about 4500 BCE, however, they began farming. As they became more settled, they also started raising livestock and making pottery. Some two thousand years later, the early Welsh learned to make tools, weapons, and jewelry out of gold and copper.

Opposite: **Early people in Wales sometimes arranged large stones to mark the entrance to burial chambers. The Pentre Ifan burial chamber in the southeast dates to about 3500 BCE.**

A detail of a bronze shield from about 2,500 years ago. The Celtic people of this period frequently used spiral designs.

The Ancient Celts

The ancient Celts from mainland Europe arrived on the island of Great Britain about 2,500 years ago. By 50 CE, there were five distinct Celtic tribes living in present-day Wales. Many of the people of Wales are descendants of the Celts. The modern Welsh language also is based on the language the Celts spoke.

The Celts had a very structured society. The common people were ruled by a class of nobles. Druids were also of high rank. They were religious scholars who performed ceremonies to honor the Celts' many gods. The Welsh island of Anglesey was an important religious center for the Druids.

The Romans Invade

In 43 CE, a massive army of foreigners invaded Britain. They were Romans. The Roman Empire had its capital in the city

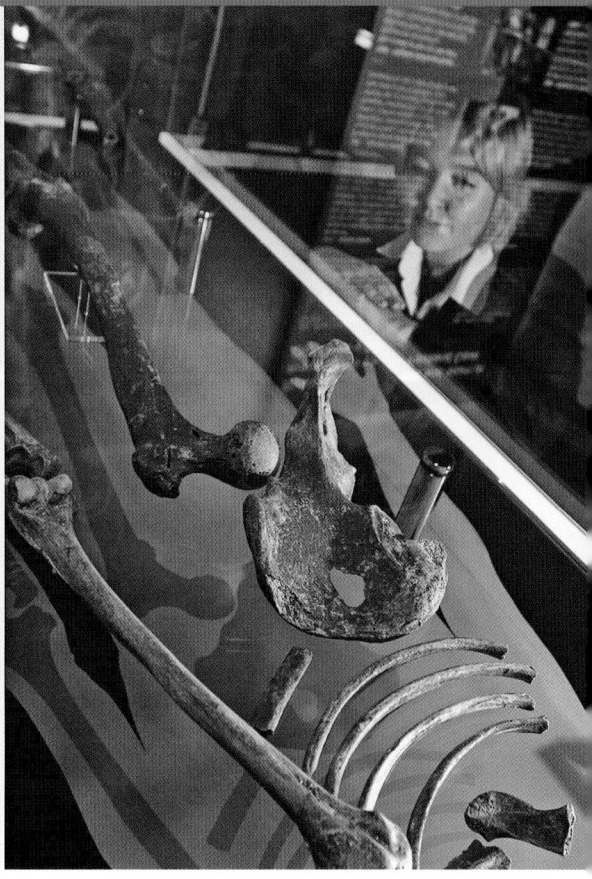

of Rome in Italy. The empire then controlled lands in Asia, Africa, and Europe. The Roman emperor Claudius wanted to expand the empire even farther west. He sent his army to take over Britain by force.

The Welsh tribes battled the invaders. The people of the island of Anglesey mounted a particularly strong defense. But the Welsh fighters were no match for the well-trained, well-armed Roman soldiers. Within a few decades, Wales was under Roman control.

To maintain their power, the Roman authorities built forts in Wales. They also constructed villas (mansions), temples, and bathhouses and introduced new goods and farming methods.

The Romans built a fortress at Caerleon in southeastern Wales. The remains of an amphitheater, now overgrown with grass, are still visible.

Some words of Latin, the language of the Roman Empire, were slowly adopted into the Welsh language.

The Romans brought a new religion to Wales—Christianity. At first, the religion was banned, and some early Welsh Christians were persecuted. But in 313 CE, the Roman emperor Constantine lifted all religious restrictions. The people of Wales were then free to worship as they wanted. By about 400 CE, most of the Welsh were Christians.

Christianity's influence grew even stronger in the fifth and sixth centuries. This era in Britain became known as the age of the saints. (A saint is a person deemed especially holy by the Catholic Church after his or her death.) During this time, leading Welsh Christians, including St. David, established monasteries that served as great centers of learning.

Becoming Welsh

By the early fifth century, the Roman Empire was no longer strong enough to maintain control over Britain. After the Romans withdrew from Wales, several kingdoms, led by princes, developed. They fought with one another for power over the region.

But they also faced an outside threat. Angles and Saxons from Europe began to invade eastern and southern Britain. Welsh leaders, though, fought hard to keep these tribes out of their realms. According to legend, one of these leaders was King Arthur, who is said to have battled the Saxons in the sixth century.

During these conflicts, the Welsh began to think of themselves as a unique people. Even if they were not united under one ruler, they did share a language, a religion, and the same enemies. The Welsh started calling themselves Cymry, which meant "fellow countrymen." At the same time, the Saxons began referring to them as Welsh, which probably translated to "foreigners."

Coming Together

In the ninth century, the Welsh faced down another invading force. These foreigners came not from the land, but from the sea. Viking pirates sailing from Scandinavia began attacking the coast of Wales. To fight the Vikings, the Welsh came together under the rule of Rhodri Mawr, or Rhodri the Great. But this united Wales did not last long. After Rhodri's death, power was again divided, falling to his various sons.

Beaumaris Castle (1295)
Conwy Castle (1283)
Flint Castle (1277)
Caernarfon Castle (1283)
Criccieth Castle (1230)
Harlech Castle (1282)
Powis Castle (1283)
Offa's Dyke
Hay Castle (late 11th century)
Grosmont Castle (1070)
Tretower Castle (early 12th century)
Pembroke Castle (1093)
Caerphilly Castle (1268)
Chepstow Castle (1067)
St. Donat's Castle (late 12th century)
Cardiff Castle (late 11th century)

Castles

The next century saw the rise of Hywel Dda, or Hywel the Good. Hywel reigned over much of Wales for more than forty years. He is best remembered for creating a standardized system of laws for Wales. After Hywel died in 950, political power was once again divided among numerous warring princes.

Fighting for Their Land

In 1066, William of Normandy, a French duke, conquered England. As the new king of England, he did not stage a full-scale invasion of Wales. He granted lands along the border between England and Wales to loyal lords. They built hundreds of castles in this border area, which was called the Welsh March. Eventually, the Marcher lords held sway over much of southeast and southwest Wales. The Welsh to the north, however, remained wholly independent of England.

During the thirteenth century, a Welsh king in northwestern Wales began extending his influence. This king, Llywelyn ap Iorwerth, sometimes called Llywelyn the Great, eventually became so powerful that Henry III, a fairly weak

English king, formally recognized him as the ruler of Wales. He was succeeded by a son and then a grandson, Llywelyn ap Gruffydd, also known as Llywelyn the Last. In the 1267 Treaty of Montgomery, Henry III gave Llywelyn the Last the title Prince of Wales. Llywelyn, in turn, acknowledged Henry as his king.

Over the course of his life, Llywelyn the Great gradually gained control of most of Wales.

Henry III died in 1272, and his son Edward I became the new king. Unlike his father, Edward did not respect Llywelyn's authority in Wales. His army invaded Wales to unite all of Britain under his rule. In 1282, Llywelyn died in battle, and Wales was conquered.

The English Take Control

To hold on to his power, Edward I embarked on a huge building project. He constructed castles in strategic places throughout Wales. In one Welsh castle, his son, who would become Edward II, was born in 1284. Edward gave the boy the title Prince of Wales. Ever since, this title has been passed on to the eldest son of the British king or queen.

Under English rule, towns emerged. Wealthy landowners had great estates, with their land worked by peasant farmers. But the impoverished Welsh never forgot the loss of their independence and resented living under English law. In the early fifteenth century, they rallied behind the Welsh rebel leader Owain Glyndwr, who declared himself the Prince of Wales. But the rebels were defeated by the English forces, ending any hope for a free Wales.

Before the century was out, Welsh soldiers went to battle in support of a would-be English king. During the Wars of the Roses, two families battled each other for the throne. The Welsh sided with Henry Tudor, whose father was from a wealthy Welsh family. With the support of the Welsh, Tudor defeated King Richard III in 1485. He took the throne as Henry VII, becoming the first king of England with Welsh blood.

Uniting England and Wales

During the reign of Henry VIII, the political ties between the English and the Welsh became more formal. What are now called the Acts of Union, enacted between 1536 and 1543, made both groups equal citizens under the law. Thereafter, the Welsh were entitled to have their own representatives in Parliament, England's lawmaking body.

But the acts also abolished the Welsh legal system. The people of Wales now had to obey English laws. English also became the official language of the government and courts in

Henry VII holds a red rose, the symbol of the English ruling family called the House of Lancaster. The symbol of the rival branch, called the House of York, was a white rose.

With so many grand castles dotting the Welsh countryside, the sixteenth-century manor house at St. Fagans, if left alone, might not have seemed like anything special. But beginning in 1948, its grounds were transformed into an extraordinary park and museum. Some forty buildings from different historical periods have been transported there and rebuilt. For visitors, a stroll through the grounds is like walking through Welsh history.

One notable building is Llys Llywelyn, which served as the royal court of a thirteenth-century Welsh prince. Another is the Kennixton Farmhouse, which dates from the seventeenth century. Its walls were painted red to ward off evil spirits. Built in 1917, the Oakdale Workmen's Institute was a social and cultural center for coal miners and their families.

St. Fagans features workshops where visitors can inspect looms (right) and watch contemporary artisans make traditional crafts. It also hosts music and dance festivals that celebrate the unique heritage of the Welsh people.

Wales. As a result, Welsh people could be tried in courts in which they could not understand the language being spoken.

Making English the official language of Wales also made an already growing gulf in Welsh society worse. Most ordinary Welsh people spoke only Welsh. Wealthy landowners, however, were likely to know English. This knowledge gave them more political power than ever before.

A New State Religion

Henry VIII also made a radical change in his subjects' religious life. The official religion in Britain had been Roman

Catholicism, a branch of Christianity. But Henry VIII wanted to divorce his wife, which the Catholic Church did not allow.

So that he could do as he pleased, the king made the Anglican Church, or the Church of England, the new state religion of England and Wales. Suddenly, the Welsh were expected to convert from Catholicism to Anglicanism.

Henry VIII also moved to close the Catholic monasteries of Wales. The king confiscated the church lands and had many valuable artworks destroyed. His actions were a blow to the culture of Wales, where monasteries had been centers of learning and scholarship.

Many monastery buildings fell to ruin after Henry VIII shut them down. The ruins of Tintern Abbey, which had been founded in 1131, still stand in southeastern Wales.

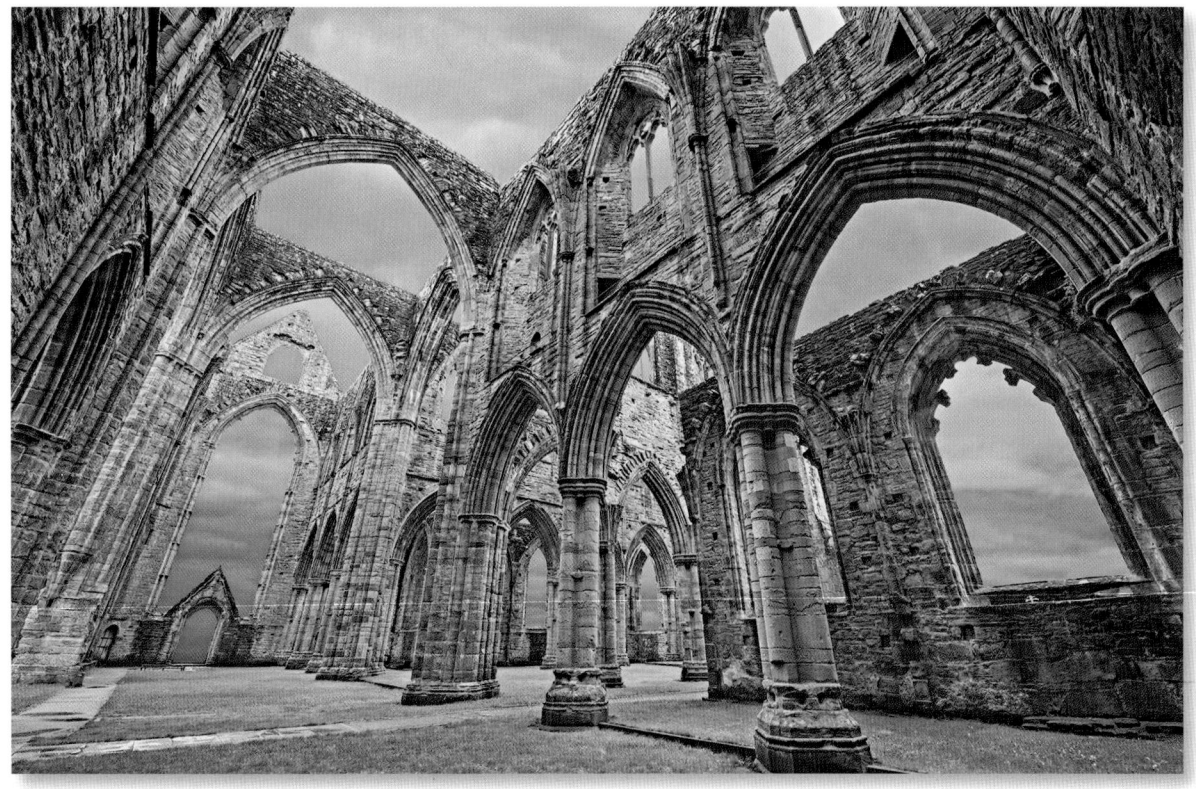

Iolo Morganwg

In his day, Iolo Morganwg was celebrated for collecting and preserving ancient Welsh literature and traditions. Morganwg was born Edward Williams in 1747. The son of a stonemason, he became a self-taught expert on history and the Welsh language.

He began writing works about these subjects, including "Gorsedd Beirdd Ynys Prydain" ("The Gorsedd of Bards of the Isles of Britain"). According to Morganwg, the Gorsedd were guardians of the Welsh songs and poetry of the ancient Celts. Morganwg also revived a Gorsedd initiation rite.

By his death in 1826, Morganwg was revered for his contributions to Welsh culture. At the time, many Welsh people were angry that the English did not seem to respect their language and culture. The stories Morganwg told of great Welsh literary traditions helped give the Welsh a sense of pride.

In the early twentieth century, however, scholars discovered that Morganwg had made up his stories of

the Gorsedd. Even though he was a fraud, Morganwg is still credited with creating a feeling of unity among the Welsh. Today, the National Eisteddfod, an annual poetry and singing competition, concludes with his Gorsedd rite.

The Nonconformists

Some Welsh still did not want to become Anglicans. They joined other Christian faiths, such as the Baptist and Congregationalist religions. People who embraced these faiths were called Nonconformists because they did not "conform" to the state church.

In the mid-1700s, several dynamic preachers began to spread another Nonconformist religion—Methodism. This faith told people to strive to live a moral life and perform good works for others. Methodism began within the Anglican Church but soon became a separate denomination.

As more Welsh people joined the Methodist Church, they built chapels in communities throughout Wales. The chapels became the focus of village social life, and ministers became leaders in their communities. By the mid-1800s, about nine out of ten Welsh people attended Nonconformist services.

Coal mines sprouted across southern Wales in the nineteenth century. In 1840, Wales produced about 4.5 million tons of coal. By 1874, it was producing about four times that amount.

The Industrial Revolution

The mid-eighteenth century also saw great changes in the Welsh economy. Traditionally, most Welsh people had made their living off the land. They farmed and raised livestock, particularly cattle and sheep. Nearly everyone lived in a rural community. In fact, there were no true cities at the time. The largest towns, such as Carmarthen and Wrexham, had only a few thousand residents.

But that all changed when new mining technologies were introduced in Wales. Quickly, iron and coal mining

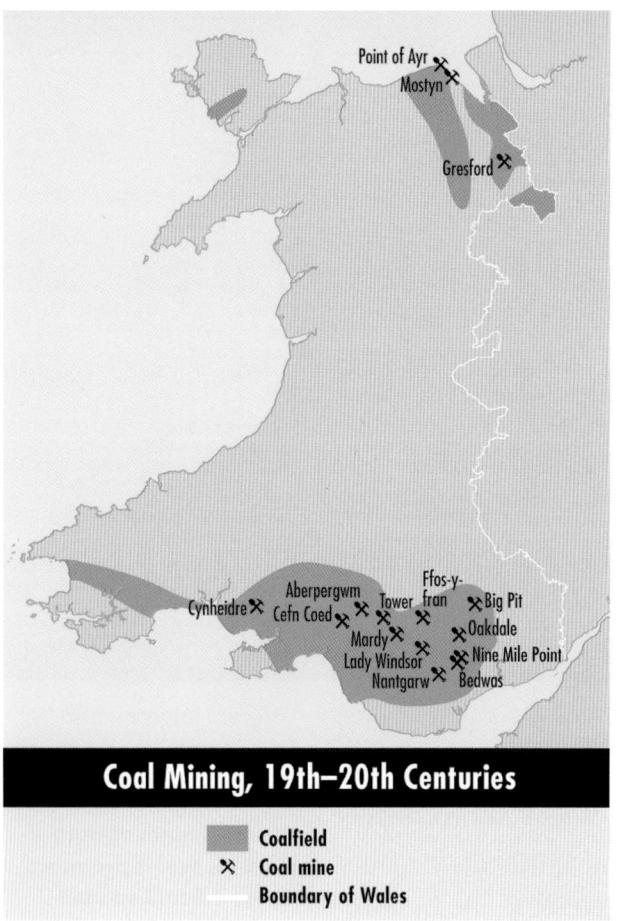

Coal Mining, 19th–20th Centuries

Point of Ayr
Mostyn
Gresford
Cynheidre
Aberpergwm
Cefn Coed
Tower
Ffos-y-fran
Big Pit
Mardy
Oakdale
Lady Windsor
Nine Mile Point
Nantgarw
Bedwas

Coalfield
Coal mine
Boundary of Wales

became vital to Wales's economy. Mining began in the northeast, but soon focused on the valleys in the south, where there were huge deposits of coal.

Coal fueled the furnaces used to make iron. The town of Merthyr Tydfil in southern Wales became home to some of the largest ironworks in the world. Ships, and later railroads, transported its iron south to ports, where it was shipped to other countries.

Soon Wales's iron mines were exhausted. The nation then started producing and exporting more coal. Coal was needed to fuel the British Industrial Revolution of the late eighteenth and early nineteenth centuries. Burning coal created steam power used to operate the large factories, locomotives, and steamships that were rapidly changing British life.

A New Way of Life

In Wales, the Industrial Revolution produced great shifts in how people made their livings. By the mid-nineteenth century, only a third of the population still worked in agriculture. The majority of men, and some boys, instead became employees of mining companies.

The Industrial Revolution also changed where people

lived. When mines opened, workers from all over Wales moved to new urban centers in the south. Cardiff, Swansea, and Newport—today Wales's three largest cities—all developed as seaports that served the iron and coal industries. The Welsh population had been scattered across the countryside. Now it became largely concentrated in southern Wales.

The population also grew larger. From 1750 to 1925, the number of people in Wales increased by five times. Because the mineral industries needed workers, immigrants from many countries arrived during this time. The Welsh now shared their land with people from England, Ireland, Spain, and Italy. Port cities also attracted sailors from around the world.

The coal industry and trade turned Newport into a thriving city by the early twentieth century.

Fighting Power

Coal mining brought many jobs to Wales. But they were largely low-paying and physically difficult. Miners labored long hours in dank tunnels, breathing unhealthy amounts of

Coal mining was hard, dirty work. Miners used picks to cut pieces of coal from the wall.

coal dust. The mines were also dangerous. Accidents were common and often resulted in death.

The living conditions in the towns around the mines were equally grim. Mining companies threw together housing for their workers. The houses were often built in terraces along the sides of the valleys where the coal was dug. Many people were crowded into a single house. The air and nearby water supplies were dirty. When disease struck these communities, it spread quickly, leaving misery and death in its wake.

Miners often banded together to demand better working and living conditions. They staged strikes, during which they refused to work until things changed. In 1898, workers formed the South Wales Miners' Federation, popularly known as the Fed. This union negotiated with mining companies on the workers' behalf.

Miners and ironworkers also fought for voting rights. They were angry because only men who owned property were allowed to vote. In 1839, five thousand workers descended on Newport. They demanded a charter of reforms that would give men who did not own property the right to cast a ballot. The Chartist riot ended when police shot at the protesters, killing more than twenty people.

The British government showed little concern about the complaints of the Welsh people. In fact, when it issued several reports about the education system in Wales, it blamed the Welsh for their own troubles. The reports, called the *Treason of the Blue Books in Wales*, said that the Welsh were backward, lazy, and immoral. The report also insisted that their use of the Welsh language made them inferior. The anti-Welsh prejudice of the Blue Books enraged the Welsh people. Many worried that their lives would never improve under British rule.

The World Wars

Despite these tensions, the Welsh fully supported the British war effort during World War I (1914–1918). About forty thousand Welsh military personnel died in the conflict. Wales also provided much needed food and coal during the war, helping to fuel a wartime economic boom.

After the war, however, the Welsh fell on hard times. The market for coal dipped, leaving many coal miners without jobs. Rural Welsh families suffered from a steep drop in food prices. During the Great Depression of the 1930s, the unemployment rate in Wales rose even higher.

From 1939 to 1945, Welsh soldiers once again took to the battlefield in World War II. Much of the city of Swansea was destroyed by bombs dropped by the German army. The United Kingdom and its allies won the war. But Wales once again suffered greatly in the postwar economic climate.

The demand for coal plunged, as electricity and natural gas became more popular energy sources. The government-run National Coal Board took over the mining industry but could not save it. Many mines closed, and the jobs they generated disappeared. At the same time, big businesses took over agriculture. Most small farmers and ranchers could no longer make a decent living.

Making a Better Wales

Wales tried to build new industries that manufactured goods such as chemicals, plastics, and electrical equipment. But even so, in the twentieth century, large numbers of young workers could not find jobs in Wales. They had to move to other countries to get work.

As Wales struggled, some Welsh people fought for more

independence from the British government. The Plaid Cymru (Party of Wales), founded in 1925, became an important political party. It wanted Wales to be allowed to govern itself. The party also promoted use of the Welsh language. Although Plaid Cymru did not send many representatives to Parliament, it brought attention to problems and issues affecting Wales.

Those seeking self-government for Wales did achieve some victories. In 1942, the British government allowed the Welsh language to be used in courts in Wales. In 1955, Cardiff became the official capital of Wales. And in 1964, the post of Secretary of State for Wales was added to the cabinet of the British national government.

Two Disasters

In the 1960s, several events made the Welsh question how much the British government cared about their future. One occurred in the village of Capel Celyn in 1965. The government made plans to build a reservoir that would flood the village. Many Welsh people objected. Not only would the project force seventy people to abandon their homes, but the reservoir was not even being built to benefit the Welsh. Instead, it would provide water to the English city of Liverpool. Welsh protesters spoke out against the project, but the British Parliament approved it anyway.

The next year, a small mining village called Aberfan suffered a horrible disaster. Waste from a nearby mine fell like a mudslide on the village. It destroyed homes and an elementary school. More than 140 people died, including 116 children. An investigation of the accident found that the government's National Coal Board was to blame. The board had been told that the situation at the mine was dangerous, but it had done nothing about the problem.

A Government for the Welsh

The flooding of Capel Celyn and the Aberfan disaster inspired many Welsh activists to push for political reforms. They fought for devolution—the passing of some powers of the British government to a new assembly of representatives in Wales. In 1979 the Welsh went to the polls to vote on devolution. But by a margin of four-to-one, the Welsh voters rejected the measure.

Devolution supporters were disappointed. But they did

not give up. They continued their fight until 1997, when another vote on devolution was held. By then, many Welsh people were angry that the British government, then under the Conservative Party, was not serving them well. With this change in the political tide, the devolution referendum passed, though narrowly. Just over half of Welsh voters called for the creation of the National Assembly for Wales.

In May 1999, the National Assembly met for the first time, marking a new chapter in Wales's history. As Wales entered the twenty-first century, it faced many challenges, from an unsteady economy to a poor transportation system to a lack of good jobs. But, with the assembly in place, the Welsh no longer had to look to politicians in faraway London for solutions to their problems. For the first time in centuries, the Welsh faced a future that they themselves could control.

CHAPTER 5

A New Government

A s part of the United Kingdom, Wales is ruled as a parliamentary constitutional monarchy. The monarch, Queen Elizabeth II, is the head of state. But the real government power rests with the prime minister and the British Parliament. The prime minister is responsible for the day-to-day running of the national government. Parliament is charged with making laws that apply to all citizens of the United Kingdom.

Opposite: **Carwyn Jones (holding mic) became the first minister of Wales in 2009.**

The Government of Wales

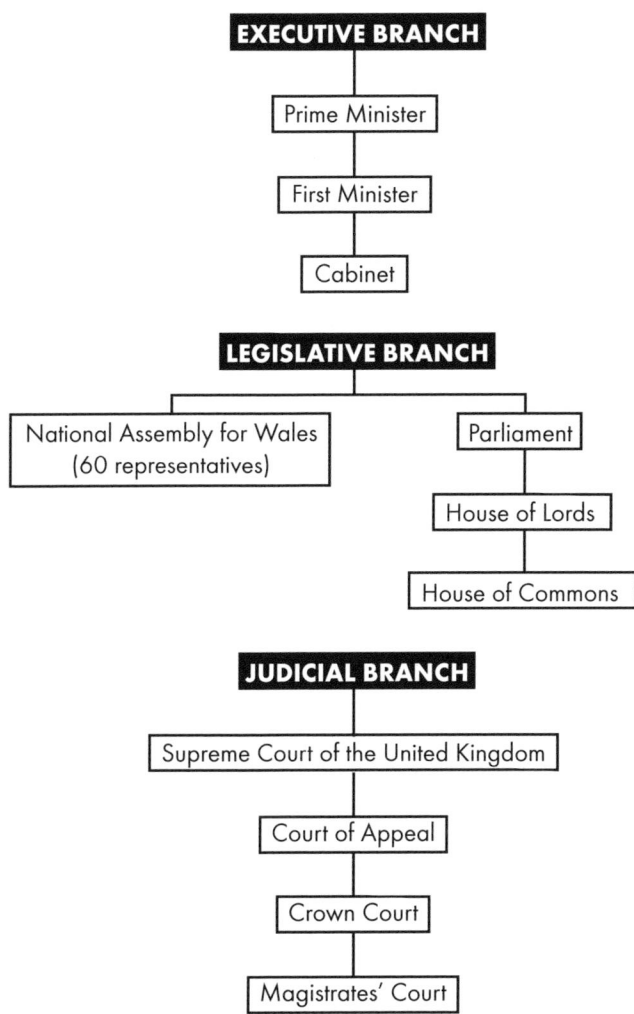

Since 1999, the Welsh people have also had their own government. Its leader is the first minister, and its lawmaking body is the National Assembly for Wales. In recent years, many powers once held by the British Parliament have been passed on to the National Assembly for Wales.

The British Parliament

The British Parliament meets in London, England. It is made up of two houses—the House of Lords and the House of Commons. Traditionally, the members of the House of Lords were wealthy people who inherited their positions. Because of recent reforms, most of its nearly eight hundred members are now appointed by Queen Elizabeth on the advice of the prime minister.

There are 650 members of Parliament, or MPs, in the House of Commons. Each MP represents a certain area, called a constituency, in the United Kingdom. Wales has forty constituencies, so it sends forty representatives to Parliament. Welsh people go to the polls every five years to elect their MP. Every British citizen in Wales who is eighteen or older is eligible to vote. Sixteen- and seventeen-year-olds are allowed to vote in local elections.

Queen Elizabeth II greets children on a visit to Wales.

A Welsh Prime Minister

David Lloyd George is the only Welsh politician to serve as the prime minister, the head of government in the United Kingdom.

Lloyd George was born in 1863 in Manchester, England. When he was a baby, his father died suddenly, leaving his mother in poverty. She moved her family to the Welsh town of Llanystumdwy to live with her brother.

With his uncle's support, Lloyd George became a lawyer. He won the admiration of his neighbors by representing tenant farmers in disputes with powerful landlords. In 1890, Lloyd George entered politics. A member of the Liberal Party, he won a seat in the House of Commons.

As an MP, Lloyd George became known for his quick wit and skill as a speaker. He helped spearhead reforms to help the poor and needy, including the elderly and the unemployed. One of his most important achievements was legislation that gave all citizens health insurance.

In 1916 Lloyd George became the prime minister.

During his tenure, World War I concluded with a British victory. He helped negotiate the Treaty of Versailles, which formally ended the conflict.

Lloyd George resigned as prime minister in 1922. He remained in the House of Commons until his death in 1945. A small museum in his hometown of Llanystumdwy commemorates his life and work.

Candidates for MP may run as independents, but most belong to a political party. In the 2017 parliamentary election, the Welsh Labour Party—long the most popular political party in Wales—won twenty-eight seats in the House of Commons. Other Welsh political parties that sent MPs to London were the Welsh Conservative Party (eight) and Plaid Cymru (four).

The parliamentary election also determines who becomes prime minister. Voters do not choose the prime minister directly. Instead, he or she is the leader of the party with the most MPs. Only once in the history of the United Kingdom has a Welsh politician been the prime minister. Welshman David Lloyd George served in that post from 1916 to 1922.

Prime ministers are assisted by the ministers they appoint to their cabinet. Each minister heads a department that oversees certain issues. For instance, there are ministers in charge of foreign affairs, health, and transportation. The Secretary of State for Wales is a cabinet position. This official ensures that the government in London addresses issues and concerns of specific importance to Wales.

Labour Party candidate Anna McMorrin celebrates her election to the British Parliament in 2017. About a quarter of the Welsh members of Parliament are women.

"Land of My Fathers"

The official national anthem of the United Kingdom is "God Save the Queen." But before soccer games and rugby matches, the Welsh prefer to sing the unofficial anthem of Wales, "Land of My Fathers."

The music was composed in 1856 by a harpist named Evan James. His father, James James, then wrote Welsh lyrics for three verses and the chorus. The tradition of singing "Land of My Fathers" at sporting events began in 1905. Before a match with a New Zealand team, Welsh rugby players loudly sang the song as a rallying cry, hoping it would rattle the rival players.

The anthem today is always sung in Welsh. It celebrates many of the things the people of Wales love most—poetry, music, their land, and their language.

Welsh lyrics

Mae hen wlad fy nhadau yn annwyl i mi.
Gwlad beirdd a chantorion, enwogion o fri,
Ei gwrol ryfelwyr, gwladgarwyr tra mad,
Tros ryddid gollasant eu gwaed.

Gwlad! Gwlad! pleidiol wyf im gwlad!
Tra mor yn fur ir bur hoff bau,
O bydded ir heniaith barhau.

English translation

The land of my fathers is dear to me.
The land of poets and singers, people of renown,
Brave warriors and patriots
Who for freedom shed their blood.

Land! Land! I am faithful to my land!
As long as the sea walls off this pure, beloved land,
May the old language endure.

A dramatic wooden funnel rises above the debating chamber of the National Assembly.

The National Assembly

Every four years, the Welsh also vote for their representatives in the National Assembly. This government body is made up of sixty representatives, called assembly members. It meets in the Welsh capital of Cardiff in a building known as the Senedd, which opened in 2006.

During an assembly election, voters cast two ballots. One vote is for a candidate running in the voter's local constituency. These constituency elections fill forty assembly seats. In each constituency, the candidate who wins the most votes becomes that area's assembly member.

Each voter also casts a vote to select an assembly member from his or her region. The five regions are North Wales, Mid and West Wales, South Wales East, South Wales West, and South Wales Central. Four members are elected from each region, for a total of twenty members.

For centuries, the dragon has been a symbol of the Welsh people. Not surprisingly, this mythical creature is found on their official flag. The top of the flag is white and the bottom half green. Spread across the flag is a large, red, winged dragon, with its right paw raised, its tail twisted, and its mouth open, revealing its pointed tongue.

The dragon has a long history in Wales. During Roman times, Roman forces sometimes marched into battle with a war flag in the shape of a dragon. Many local leaders in Great Britain adopted the dragon as their symbol, including the legendary King Arthur. When Owain Glyndwr revolted against the English, he raised a dragon flag.

The current colors of the Welsh flag date to the reign of Henry Tudor, who was of Welsh descent. In 1485, with the help of the Welsh, he became the king of England after defeating Richard III at the Battle of Bosworth Field. His battle flag combined the red dragon as a Welsh symbol with green and white, the traditional military colors of Wales.

In the 1950s, the English government barred the flag from a celebration of St. David's Day, honoring Wales's patron saint. The Welsh people were outraged. Under pressure from the Gorsedd, an important Welsh cultural society, Queen Elizabeth II declared the Welsh red dragon the official flag of Wales in 1959. It now flies high over the Senedd, the building where Wales's National Assembly meets.

In elections for regional members, people do not vote for a candidate. Instead, they vote for a political party. Each party makes up a ranked list of people it wants to send to the Assembly. The number of votes a party gets determines how many seats it gets to fill in each region.

In the 2016 election, the Labour Party won twenty-nine Assembly seats. Voters gave Plaid Cymru twelve seats, the Conservative Party eleven seats, the UK Independence Party (UKIP) seven seats, and the Liberal Democrats one seat.

Vaughan Gething, a member of the Welsh Assembly from Cardiff, is the cabinet secretary for health, well-being, and sport. In this position, he is responsible for the management of the national health system.

Governing Wales

The British Parliament still makes laws in certain areas—including taxation, foreign policy, and defense—that apply to the Welsh. But in 2011 the Assembly was given the right to make laws dealing with other aspects of government. These now include economic development; education and training; health and health services; tourism; culture; and the Welsh language. The laws passed by the Assembly apply to Wales, but to nowhere else in the United Kingdom.

The executive branch in Wales is called the Welsh Government. It implements the laws and policies of the National Assembly. The Welsh Government is led by the first minister. This official is formally appointed by the monarch after being nominated by the assembly members. Since the Welsh Government was established, it has had three first ministers—Alun Michael, Rhodri Morgan, and Carwyn Jones.

The first minister is responsible for choosing the cabinet. It is made up of ministers, deputy ministers, and the counsel

Wales's Capital

Cardiff is one of the youngest capital cities in Europe. Located in south Wales, it was a small town until it became the nation's busiest port during the eighteenth and nineteenth centuries. Cardiff officially became a city in 1905. Only fifty years later, it was formally named the capital of Wales. Today, it has a population of about 345,000.

Cardiff is the economic, educational, and cultural center of Wales. It is home to the main campus of the University of Wales as well as several other colleges. The National Museum of Wales in Cardiff features an extensive collection of European art.

One of Cardiff's most notable landmarks is Cardiff Castle, located at the city's center. A Norman lord built the castle in the eleventh century at the site of an old Roman fort. The city's waterfront is another important attraction. Tourists and residents alike gather at the shops and restaurants that line the shore of Cardiff Bay.

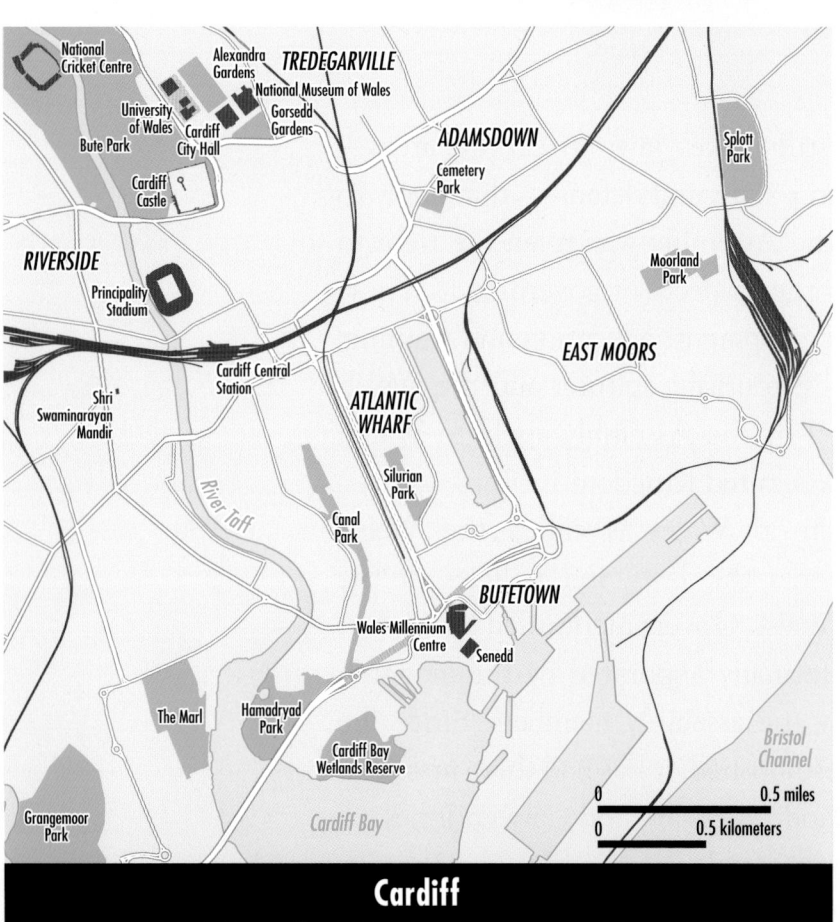

Cardiff

general. The ministers, with the help of the deputy ministers, are in charge of specific areas of governance. The counsel general provides legal advice to the Welsh Government.

The Welsh people are also subject to their local governments. Wales is divided into twenty-two areas called unitary authorities. Each unitary authority has a council. These councils deal with local issues, such as housing and road upkeep. They are funded by grants from the federal government and sometimes by local taxes.

The Judicial System

The United Kingdom has three separate judicial systems: One is for Scotland, one is for Northern Ireland, and one is for England and Wales.

Most court cases are first tried in lower courts. Cases involving family issues are heard in Family Court. The majority of civil cases are sent to County Court. Criminal cases and some civil cases are tried in Magistrates' Court. Some more serious criminal matters, however, are sent directly to a higher court, known as Crown Court.

Once cases are decided, they can be challenged in an appeal. Appeals are first heard by the Crown Court or High Court. They can then be appealed to the Court of Appeal and finally to the Supreme Court of the United Kingdom, the highest court in the land. First established in 2009, it only hears a select number of cases. The cases chosen are likely to have an impact not just on the legal system, but on British society as well.

CHAPTER 6

Making a Living

Until recently, the modern Welsh economy was powered by coal. Most of its laborers worked in the great mines in the south. But when demand for coal dropped in the twentieth century, the mines began to close. The last coal mine was shut down in 2008, marking the end of mining as Wales's main economic driver.

The Welsh people have worked hard to create new types of jobs to replace those lost in mining. Because of this effort, the unemployment rate in Wales today hovers around 5 percent, only slightly higher than the rest of the United Kingdom. Most people in Wales now work in the manufacturing and service industries. But a few rural people continue to live off the land by farming crops, catching fish, and raising livestock.

Opposite: **Wales has three times as many sheep as people. It is home to more sheep than any of the other three parts of the United Kingdom.**

Agriculture, Fishing, and Forestry

In much of Wales, the land is unsuitable for farming crops because of its poor soil and high elevation. The exception is the southern coastal plain and the island of Anglesey. Most Welsh farms are located there. These farms produce wheat, barley, potatoes, and oats for animal feed.

The grasslands of the Welsh countryside also provide food for livestock. Many rural workers in central Wales raise sheep both for meat and for wool. Cattle, too, are raised for meat, while dairy cows produce milk. Wales's dairy industry is centered in the southwest.

The Welsh government has invested heavily in reforesting its wilderness lands. Its Forestry Commission maintains large forests, which are used to produce timber.

Some commercial fishers ply their trade in Wales's coastal waters. Working in small fishing vessels, they haul in catches of lobsters, cod, and skate.

Combined, the farming, forestry, and fishing industries are only a small part of the Welsh economy. They account for just 2 percent of the gross domestic product (GDP), the total value of the goods Wales produces each year.

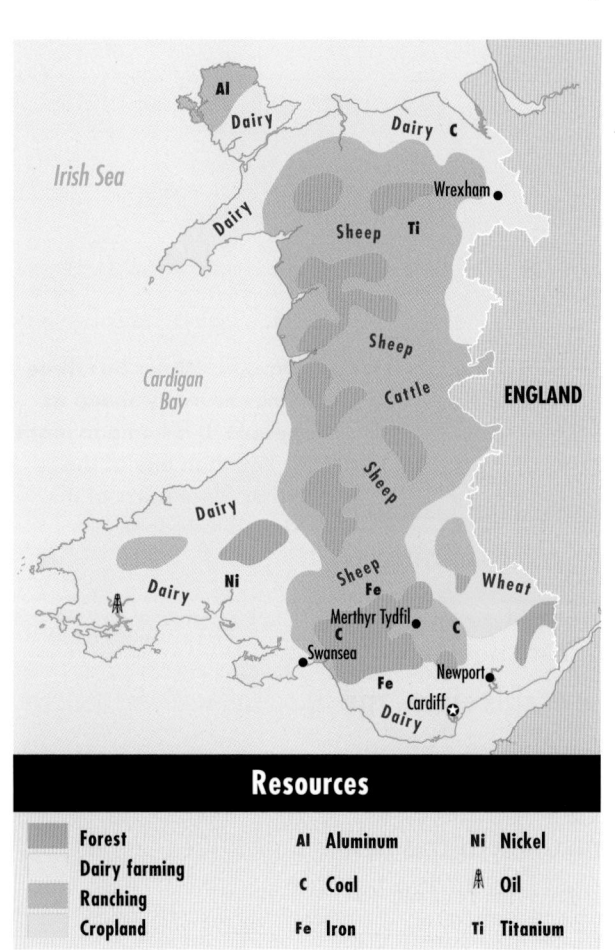

Resources

▨ Forest	Al	Aluminum	Ni Nickel
Dairy farming	C	Coal	⚒ Oil
Ranching			
Cropland	Fe	Iron	Ti Titanium

Making Goods

When the coal mines were shutting down, Wales tried to encourage companies to move manufacturing plants there. Manufacturing now makes up about one-third of the economy.

Several automobile companies, including Ford and Toyota, have factories in Wales. Workers manufacture engines and other car parts. In 2016, the British luxury car brand Aston Martin chose Wales as the site of a factory to produce SUVs. Now about seventeen thousand people in Wales work in automotive manufacturing.

Other important manufacturing products include optoelectronics. Welsh factories in this industry make lasers, sensors, solar cells, and fiber optics. Plants in Wales also produce chemicals, plastics, and metals such as tinplate and steel.

Welsh lobstermen remove a crab from a trap. The trap will then be baited with fish and returned to the sea.

What Wales Grows, Makes, and Mines

AGRICULTURE (2015)

Wheat	1,764,000 metric tons
Mutton and lamb	64,672 metric tons
Eggs	532,000,000 eggs

MANUFACTURING

Cement (2013)	400,000 metric tons
Iron (2016)	3,470,000 metric tons
Steel (2016)	4,480,000 metric tons

MINING (2013)

Coal	2,400,000 metric tons
Crushed rock	12,300,000 metric tons
Sand and gravel	1,700,000 metric tons

Service and Tourism Jobs

The majority of Welsh workers hold jobs in service industries. They work in retail sales, education, health care, and government, among other fields. Wales is working to expand its financial and insurance industries, but they are growing slowly.

Many service jobs are part of the tourism industry. About one hundred thousand people work at hotels, restaurants, museums, and attractions. Visitors to Wales now spend about $6.5 billion there each year. Many come from other places in the United Kingdom, especially London. But Wales also attracts international tourists from the United States, Canada, and other countries in Europe.

Tourists often travel to Wales to bask in its natural beauty. Wales's three national parks are popular destinations. The coastline also attracts visitors with its dramatic cliffs and sandy beaches. Dedicated hikers can take in the sights of the Wales Coast Path, which meanders along 870 miles (1,400 km) of coastline.

Wales's historic buildings are also a draw. The nation has some six hundred castles—some left in ruins, but others restored to their original glory. All have fascinating stories that hold special appeal to history buffs. Visitors are also attracted to the beautiful chapels and ornate churches found throughout the country.

Wales and the European Union

Another important aspect of Wales's economy is the United Kingdom's membership in the European Union (EU). The EU is an international organization made up of many European countries. Members of the EU can freely trade goods with one

A chef carefully assembles a dish at his restaurant in western Wales. Many Welsh restaurants are attracting visitors by showcasing local ingredients.

Bounce Below

With the decline of the mineral industries, many Welsh mines were abandoned. Recently, several have been revamped as tourist attractions. For example, an old slate mine in northern Wales has been transformed into Bounce Below. Outfitted in jumpsuits and helmets, visitors take a train deep into the underground mine. There, giant nets are installed, creating enormous trampolines. The trampolines are connected by slides that send guests flying from one level to another. While everyone bounces and slides, an LED light show fills the strange cavernous playground with bright, pulsating colors.

another. EU citizens also can easily move to any EU country and work there.

For Wales, belonging to the EU has had some major economic benefits. Because of the free trade agreements, companies from all over Europe have made business investments in Wales. Wales also receives sizable funding from the EU. In 2016, Wales paid £414 million ($548 million) into the EU, but it got back £658 million ($870 million). EU funds help to support many poorer communities. About 80 percent of rural farmers are kept afloat by money they receive from the EU.

Brexit and Beyond

In recent years, some British people began to feel that belonging to the European Union was hurting their economy, not helping it. Others were not comfortable with immigrants from other European nations coming to the United Kingdom. The United Kingdom held a referendum, or vote, on whether or not the UK should remain in the European Union.

Carwyn Jones, Wales's first minister, campaigned against Brexit—the nickname for a British exit from the EU. But when the vote was taken on June 23, 2016, 53 percent of the Welsh voted to leave. The English also voted to leave, while Scotland and Northern Ireland voted to remain. The total vote in favor of exiting the European Union was high enough that the referendum passed.

The outcome was a surprise, and the economic consequences of the Brexit vote are not clear. As the British government negotiates its EU exit, many Welsh people are worrying about Wales's economic future. Will foreign companies stop investing in Wales? Will goods exported by Wales be subject to high taxes? Will the British government step up to replace the EU funds Wales will lose? In the coming years, Brexit is likely to reshape Wales's economy, but exactly how is not yet known.

CHAPTER 7

Welsh People and Language

ROUGHLY THREE MILLION PEOPLE LIVE IN WALES. About four out of five of them live in urban areas. Most of the population is clustered in the northeast and in the south. The rest of Wales is sparsely populated.

Opposite: **An elderly Welsh man looks out over the landscape. On average, Welsh people live eighty years.**

Natives and Immigrants

Most of the Welsh—about 73 percent—were born in Wales. Another 21 percent were originally from England. Only 1 percent was born in Scotland or Northern Ireland.

The number of foreign-born residents of Wales almost doubled between 2001 and 2011, so that about 5 percent of the population was born outside of the United Kingdom. Most of the recent immigrants are from Poland. Others came from India, Germany, South Africa, and the Republic of Ireland.

The overwhelming majority—about 96 percent—of the Welsh are white. Some are descendants of prehistoric people who arrived in Wales from other areas of Europe. Others

Persons per square mile		Persons per square kilometer
more than 520		more than 200
131–520		51–200
27–130		11–50
3–26		1–10
fewer than 3		fewer than 1

Population of Major Cities (2015 est.)

Cardiff	345,810
Swansea	182,361
Newport	130,086
Wrexham	62,487
Merthyr Tydfil	44,265

trace their roots to one or more groups that came to Wales later. These peoples included the Celts, Romans, Anglo-Saxons, Vikings, Normans, and English.

Wales's small non-white population includes about sixty-seven thousand people of Asian ancestry and eighteen thousand of African and Caribbean descent. Historically, the most multiethnic area in Wales is a neighborhood in Cardiff called Butetown. Also known as Tiger Bay, it was the home of sailors from around the world during Wales's coal boom.

The Importance of Welsh

In the sixteenth century, King Henry VIII made English the official language of Wales. But some Welsh never stopped speaking their native tongue. By the beginning of the twentieth century, however, the Welsh language was in danger of dying out. At that time, much of the population moved to the south to work in the coal and iron industries, where English was the common language. Increasingly, Welsh was mostly heard only in isolated rural communities.

Fearing Welsh might disappear forever, activists took up the cause of preserving the language. Founded in 1962, a group called the Welsh Language Society worked to make Welsh an official language in Wales. The organization also petitioned the British Broadcasting Corporation (BBC) to create a Welsh-language television channel.

Some activists in the Welsh language movement took a more radical approach. They vandalized road signs with words in English. In the 1970s, a group calling themselves Meibion Glyndwr (Sons of Glendower) began setting fire to vacation homes owned by English people in Welsh-speaking areas.

The protests finally pressured the British government to act. In 1967, Welsh, in addition to English, became an official language of Wales. In 1982, the BBC began broadcasting S4C,

A white man and an Asian man relax on a bench in Wales. The largest number of Welsh Asians are of Indian descent.

Ethnic Groups in Wales

White	95.6%
Asian or Asian British	2.2%
Mixed Race	1.0%
Black or Black British	0.6%
Other Ethnic Group	0.5%

Llanfairpwllgwyngyllgogerychwyrndrobwllllantysiliogogogoch is the longest place name in Europe. The town, located on the island of Anglesey, is home to about three thousand people.

a TV channel devoted to Welsh-language programs. And in 1993, the Welsh Language Act established that both English and Welsh are to be used in government business. Now all road signs and public notices are written in both languages. The 1993 act also created the Welsh Language Board to encourage use of the Welsh language. Most of its duties were transferred to the Welsh Language Commissioner in 2012.

Today, most Welsh people use English in their daily life. However, in some parts of Wales, using the Welsh language remains a point of pride and a declaration of Welsh identity.

The Languages of Wales

According to the 2011 census, nearly every Welsh household—about 97 percent—speaks either English or Welsh.

Only a small minority of recent immigrants speaks another language at home. These languages include Polish, Arabic, and Bengali, a language spoken in Bangladesh and India.

Nearly everyone in Wales can speak English. Only about 19 percent of the population can speak Welsh. About 15

Signs in Wales are in both Welsh and English.

Common Welsh Words and Phrases

Sut mae	Hello
Hwyl fawr	Good-bye
Bore da	Good morning
Nos da	Good night
Os gwelwch in dda	Please
Diolch	Thank you
Croeso	You're welcome
Sut ydych chi?	How are you?
Ie	Yes
Nage	No

Teaching the Welsh to Read

In the early eighteenth century, a Welsh minister named Griffith Jones set out on a mission to teach the Welsh people how to read. At the time, most Welsh people had little access to education. To remedy the problem, Jones set up a system of "circulating schools."

The teachers in each circulating school traveled to a village and held classes for adults and children. They arrived in the winter, when farming families had fewer chores to do. Using the Welsh Bible, the teachers spent three months teaching reading skills to as many people as possible. The teachers then left and set up the circulating school in another village.

The program was extremely successful in spreading literacy throughout Wales. After just thirty years, circulating schools had taught about half of the Welsh population to read.

percent can read and write it as well. Only about 5 percent of the population speaks Welsh exclusively, without English as a second language.

Most Welsh speakers live in western and northwestern Wales, the areas farthest from the English border. Cardiff, however, also has a large Welsh-speaking community. It is made up of people from Welsh-speaking regions who moved to the capital, often in search of jobs.

The Welsh channel S4C now broadcasts more than eighty hours of television a week. The BBC also operates Radio Cymru, a Welsh-only radio station. Welsh speakers can also get news and information from written sources, including Y Cymro, an online weekly Welsh newspaper.

Learning Welsh

In the nineteenth century, students in many English-speaking schools in Wales were terrified of the Welsh Not. The Welsh Not was a stick that teachers gave to any pupil caught speaking Welsh. The Welsh Not was a badge of shame, meant to humiliate children for speaking their people's language.

The situation is very different in Welsh schools today. Students are no longer discouraged from speaking Welsh. In fact, by law, they must study the language. Since 1999, all pupils between the ages of five and sixteen have been required to take classes in Welsh. In some schools, Welsh is the only language spoken.

Many universities in Wales teach Welsh as well. In recent years, Welsh classes have become popular not just with college students but also with older English-speaking adults. The S4C television channel has even turned learning Welsh into entertainment. On the reality show *Cariad@Iaith:Love4Language*, English-speaking celebrities take intensive Welsh classes for a week and compete to see who can best master the language.

A teacher works with children at a Welsh elementary school. Children in Wales are required to start school by age five.

CHAPTER 8

Religious Life

FOR MOST OF ITS HISTORY, WALES HAS BEEN A Christian nation. The majority of the Welsh people describe themselves as Christians. But in recent years, the number of Welsh Christians has dropped sharply. In 2001, about 72 percent of the Welsh people identified as Christian. Just ten years later, only about 58 percent did.

Other faiths are on the rise in Wales. The number of Muslims, in particular, almost doubled between 2001 and 2011. But the fastest growing religious affiliation in Wales is no religious affiliation at all. Almost one-third of all Welsh people do not belong to any religion.

That statistic reflects an important shift in how people live. Welsh communities are now much less centered on churches and chapels than they had been in the past.

Opposite: **Many old Welsh churches were built of stone.**

Wales's Patron Saint

A sixth-century Catholic priest, now known as St. David, holds a special place among the Welsh. As the patron saint of Wales, he is thought to be their divine protector.

St. David was born in southwestern Wales in about 520. The son of a prince, he traveled throughout Britain and Ireland, helping to spread the Christian faith. St. David also established numerous churches and monasteries.

St. David is credited with performing several miracles. His most famous miracle is said to have occurred during a sermon. While speaking to a crowd outside, he raised the lowland he was standing on into a high hill so everyone could see and hear him.

In 589, St. David died on March 1, which the Welsh now celebrate as St. David's Day. One of Wales's greatest churches—St. David's Cathedral in Pembrokeshire—is named in his honor.

Christian Faiths

The Romans introduced Christianity to Wales in the first century. Over time, most of the Welsh became Roman Catholics. But in the sixteenth century, King Henry VIII defied the Catholic Church and made Anglicanism (the Church of England) the official religion of united England and Wales.

Some Welsh Catholics refused to convert. Many were persecuted. More than ninety were executed for their beliefs. However, most Welsh abandoned Catholicism for Anglicanism with little resistance.

The number of Catholics in Wales dwindled until the mid-nineteenth century. At that time, Catholics from Ireland began emigrating to Wales to escape a great famine in their own land. But even with these new immigrants, the Catholic population of Wales remained small. By the beginning of the twenty-first century, about 3 percent of the Welsh population was Catholic.

Today most Welsh Christians belong to Protestant religions, such as the Methodist, Presbyterian, and Baptist churches. During the eighteenth century in Wales, these faiths became known as Nonconformist. Their followers did

The Welsh Bible

King Henry VIII persecuted Catholics in Wales who would not embrace Anglicanism. His daughter, Queen Elizabeth I, came up with a less violent way of converting Welsh Catholics. She commissioned a translation of the Bible into the Welsh language. An Anglican clergyman named William Morgan spent many years on the project. He made sure to use simple language so that ordinary Welsh people could understand and appreciate Bible verses.

After the translation was published, in 1588, Anglican church services in Wales were held in Welsh. The Welsh liked going to church and hearing their own language. (Catholic church services had been held in the ancient Roman language of Latin.)

Because of the Welsh Bible, the Welsh gradually came to accept the Anglican Church. The Bible also proved important to Welsh culture. It created a standard for written Welsh, which helped keep the language alive.

not conform with the beliefs of the Anglican Church, the official church of England and Wales.

As Nonconformists grew in number, they resented having to pay taxes to the Anglican Church. They supported the Wales Church Act of 1914. The law formally separated the Welsh Anglican Church (renamed the Church in Wales) from the Church of England. Since the act's passage, Wales has had no official state religion.

St. David's Cathedral in Pembrokeshire is one of the largest churches in Wales. It belongs to the Church in Wales denomination, which has the most followers of any religion in Wales.

In 1881, the British Parliament passed the Sunday Closing (Wales) Act. It banned Welsh pubs from selling alcohol on Sunday. Followers of Nonconformist religions, who then made up about half of the Welsh population, celebrated the law. They wanted people to spend their Sundays at religious services.

The law, which was fully repealed in 1961, did more than curb alcohol use. It also helped create a Welsh political identity. It was the first British law that applied only to Wales. The very idea that Wales could have its own laws helped inspire people to fight for their own government.

Also because of the law, many men founded private clubs, which were still allowed to serve alcohol on Sunday. These clubs became places where working-men could exchange political ideas and organize to demand higher wages.

Chapel Culture

Nonconformist faiths helped shape traditional Welsh culture. In the nineteenth and early twentieth centuries, chapels were the focus of village life. The ministers served as community leaders and as moral guardians. They often delivered fiery sermons, harshly judging anyone who strayed from a godly path.

Chapels were social as well as religious centers. People gathered there to celebrate weddings and baptisms. And every Sunday, chapels were full from morning to night. They held three services, including Sunday school, during which children listened to stories from the Bible. For many Welsh children, the highlight of the year was an annual Sunday school trip to a seaside resort.

Each year, on the day after Easter, chapels held a Cymanfa Ganu (sometimes spelled Gymanfa Ganu), or singing festival. Preparation for the event began weeks before. The chapel's congregation attended a series of practice sessions, so they all could master their singing parts.

On the day of the festival, women and girls wore brand-new outfits and straw hats. The best singers took their place at

Welsh people take part in a Cymanfa Ganu service.

the front of the chapel, so their voices could be heard loud and clear. Then together, the congregation would begin singing in four-part harmony.

The Welsh still hold Cymanfa Ganus at some chapels and festivals. But chapel culture overall has faded. Fewer people go to services each Sunday. Attendance has dropped so low that many chapels have closed down. Some have been abandoned and left in ruins. Others have been transformed into homes, shops, restaurants, and clubs.

Other Religions

Only a small minority of Welsh people observe a non-Christian religion. The largest of these is Islam. Wales is home to about forty-five thousand Muslims, or followers of Islam. Many Welsh Muslims are descendants of immigrants from Yemen, a small country in the Middle East. There are about forty mosques, Islamic houses of worship, in Wales.

Beginning in the 1730s, Jewish communities developed in several cities and towns, including Cardiff, Swansea, Merthyr Tydfil, and Tredegar. At its height, the Jewish population of

Religions of Wales	
Christian	57.6%
No religion	32.1%
Muslim	1.5%
Hindu	0.3%
Buddhist	0.3%
Sikh	0.1%
Jewish	0.1%
Other religion	0.4%
Religion not given	7.6%

A young Muslim couple walks through Swansea. Most Welsh Muslims live in cities such as Cardiff and Swansea.

Shri Swaminarayan Mandir, the first Hindu temple in Wales, opened in 1982.

Wales was almost five thousand. But the number began to drop after 1911. In that year, out-of-work miners in Tredegar took their anger out on the town's Jewish population by attacking and looting their homes and businesses. There are now only about three thousand Welsh Jews, most of whom live in Cardiff.

The ten thousand Hindus in Wales are mostly immigrants from India, Pakistan, Sri Lanka, and other Asian countries. Cardiff is home to Shri Swaminarayan Mandir, the nation's largest Hindu temple. Other religious faiths represented in Wales are Buddhism and Sikhism.

A small group of Welsh people embrace a version of Wales's oldest religious tradition—Druidry. Drawing on the beliefs of the ancient Celts and more recent texts, they look for spiritual experiences in the natural world. Every year, modern Druids gather on the island of Anglesey on the summer solstice, the longest day of the year. Wearing white robes, they hold a ceremony at dawn, during which they make offerings to the sky, the land, and the sea.

Druids take part in a ceremony on the island of Anglesey. The island has been a center of the Druid religion since Celtic times.

CHAPTER 9

Songs, Stories, and Sports

WALES HAS A RICH CULTURAL HERITAGE. Throughout history, the Welsh have displayed a deep love for poetry, storytelling, and—most of all—music and singing. Both because of its strong musical traditions and its contributions to the contemporary music scene, Wales has more than earned its nickname, the Land of Song.

Musical Traditions

The traditional music of Wales features several unique instruments. One is the *crwth*, a stringed instrument played with a bow. Another is the *pibgorn*, a type of pipe made from wood and the horns of a bull.

Opposite: **The harp is considered the national instrument of Wales.**

The pibgorn is a wooden pipe with a bull's horn at one end to blow through and a horn bell at the other end to project the sound.

But the instrument most associated with Wales is the harp. Traditional music often employs the triple harp. Resting the harp on the left shoulder, triple harpists play the high strings with the left hand and the low strings with the right.

In the Welsh singing style known as *penillion*, or *cerdd dant*, a harpist accompanies a singer. The singer chants lines of a poem while the harpist plays a song. In the past, penillion singers were usually men, but today many women have embraced the old singing style.

Hymns and Choirs

By the nineteenth century, choral singing during Sunday services became a vital part of Welsh life. With a high demand for church music, Wales produced several accomplished hymn composers, including John Hughes and Ann Griffiths. The most famous was William Williams. Today, even as fewer people are attending chapel services, the Welsh still enjoy singing Williams's hymns, especially "Guide Me, O Thou Great Jehovah." The song is a longtime favorite of crowds at rugby matches.

During the height of the coal industry in Wales, miners would often form all-male choirs. The choirs staged friendly

The Wales Millennium Centre

Since it opened in 2004, the Wales Millennium Centre has become one of the nation's most famous landmarks. Located in Cardiff, it is known affectionately as the Armadillo because of its shape and stone exterior. The unique building was constructed from materials found and made in Wales, including slate, steel, glass, and seven types of wood.

The front of the center bears a two-line bilingual inscription written by Welsh poet Gwyneth Lewis. The Welsh line reads "Creu Gwir Fel Gwydr o Ffwrnais Awen" ("Creating Truth Like Glass from the Furnace of Inspiration"). The English line reads "In These Stones Horizons Sing."

Welcoming more than 1.5 million visitors a year, the performing arts center hosts a wide variety of shows, including theater, dance, concerts, and comedy. It is also the home of the Welsh National Opera (WNO) and the WNO Orchestra and WNO Chorus.

The building itself has become something of a television star. It has appeared in several British shows, including *Dr. Who* and *Torchwood*, both of which are filmed in Cardiff.

The Mari Lwyd

The Mari Lwyd (Gray Mare) used to be a favorite Christmas tradition in Wales. During the Mari Lwyd, a group of male singers roamed through their village. One played the part of the mare by wrapping himself in cloth and holding a horse's skull on a stick above his head.

When the singers stopped at a house, they sang a request for the family to let them inside. The family and the singers then engaged in a singing competition called the *pwnco*. The two groups took turns singing insults at one another in rhyme. They often made up their jabs on the spot.

If the singers won the battle, the family invited them inside for cake and drinks. Before leaving, the singers entertained their hosts with a special farewell song.

singing contests with one another. Their love of competition led to one of the most heralded moments in Welsh musical history. In 1872, the Great Choir of the South Wales Choral Union traveled to the Crystal Palace in London to sing in a competition there. The crowd expected little from the rough-looking miners. But when they opened their mouths to sing, their beautiful voices enthralled the audience. The choir won the competition both that year and the next, sealing Wales's reputation for having extraordinary choral singers.

The tradition lives on today. Several Welsh men's choirs still tour venues throughout the world. The most famous is the Treorchy Male Choir, which was founded in a mining village in 1883.

Opera and Pop

In 1946 Wales became the first nation to have its own opera company. Since then, it has produced several heralded talents, including Gwyneth Jones and Margaret Price. Wales also celebrates opera at the Cardiff Singer of the World. Every two years, this international competition brings together many of the greatest young opera singers in the world.

Wales has also made a name for itself in popular music. In concert halls and clubs, just about any type of music can be heard—from jazz to hip-hop to electronica. Welsh recording artists often find a large audience within the United Kingdom.

A few, though, have captured even broader fame. In the 1960s, the Welsh singers Tom Jones and Shirley Bassey became international stars, lauded for their bold, full-throated

The Manic Street Preachers were famed for mixing energetic rock music with political lyrics.

Pop Star

With a career spanning six decades, Shirley Bassey is Wales's most famous and beloved pop singer.

Bassey was born to an English mother and a Nigerian father in 1937. Her family lived in Tiger Bay in the port city of Cardiff. The multicultural community welcomed people from around the world.

Bassey's family struggled to make ends meet. She quit school at fourteen and began working in a factory. On weekends, she sang at pubs and at variety shows to earn a little extra money.

Audiences were awed by Bassey's powerful voice. While still a teenager, she began playing nightclubs in London. In the late 1950s, Bassey became a frequent television guest and a recording star. She would go on to have more than two dozen hits on the charts in the United Kingdom.

Bassey had her greatest success with her rendition of theme songs for three James Bond films—"Goldfinger,"

"Diamonds Are Forever," and "Moonraker." In 2013, she sang "Goldfinger" at the Academy Awards during a James Bond tribute and received a standing ovation.

vocals. In the 1990s, several Welsh bands made a splash in the European music scene. Manic Street Preachers, Catatonia, and Stereophonics were all part of a musical movement dubbed Cool Cymru. Another important Welsh band from this period, Super Furry Animals, is known for singing a mix of Welsh and English lyrics.

Writing in Welsh and English

Wales has a long literary tradition in both of its official languages. The earliest known works of literature in Welsh date from the late sixth century. Taliesin and Aneirin were authors of praise poetry. They were hired by wealthy lords and princes to write long poems about the patrons' heroic deeds. This praise poetry tradition continued for centuries.

Dafydd ap Gwilym is one of Wales's most famous poets. Writing in the fourteenth century, ap Gwilym composed some praise poetry for wealthy patrons, but he also wrote about his own life and feelings. Many of ap Gwilym's most notable works are rich explorations of his favorite topics—love and the natural world.

Medieval Wales also produced *cyfarwyddiaid*, or professional storytellers. Some of their stories were written down and survived into modern times. These folktales were collected in the *Mabinogion*, which was published in the mid-nineteenth century. The *Mabinogion* presents a mythical fantasy world full of giants, dragons, and witches.

The story of Culhwch and Olwen is included in the *Mabinogion*. It tells of Culhwch, a prince in King Arthur's court, who marries Olwen, the daughter of the king of the giants.

By the early twentieth century, most Welsh literature was written in English, as fewer people in Wales knew Welsh. The country's most famous English-language literary figure is Dylan Thomas. He was considered one of the greatest poets of the twentieth century. His best-known works include "Do Not Go Gentle into That Good Night" and "And Death Shall Have No Dominion." He also chronicled Welsh small-town life in his famed radio plays *Under Milk Wood* and *A Child's Christmas in Wales*.

The poetry of Dylan Thomas is renowned for its mix of humor and sadness.

The Dylan Thomas Centre is located in Thomas's hometown of Swansea. Every autumn, it hosts the Dylan Thomas Festival, a two-week celebration that begins on the anniversary of his birth and ends on the anniversary of his death. Fans of the poet can also explore the Dylan Thomas Trail and see the places that inspired his work.

Roald Dahl is another famous Welsh author who wrote in English. Dahl was best known for his children's books, including *Charlie and the Chocolate Factory* and *Matilda*. Every year, Cardiff, where he was born, hosts a children's party on Dahl's birthday.

Roald Dahl wrote dark but funny books for children. They often featured evil adults who threatened the children at the heart of the story.

Art, Film, and TV

When the Welsh were largely a rural people, they were known for a variety of traditional crafts. These included glassblowing, pottery making, weaving, and needlework. But with the growth of urban centers, many Welsh people also began exploring fine arts, such as painting and sculpture.

A painting of a village by Kyffin Williams

One of best regarded Welsh artists is Ceri Richards. He was especially known for his paintings and drawings based on the works of Dylan Thomas. Another is Shani Rhys James, who is heralded for her haunting self-portraits. Perhaps the most famous Welsh painter is Kyffin Williams. A resident of the island of Anglesey, he was celebrated for his works depicting the landscapes of northern Wales.

The natural beauty of Wales has inspired many filmmakers to make movies there. *King Arthur: Legend of the Sword*, *Snow White and the Huntsman*, and *Captain America: The First Avenger* are just a few of the recent films that showcase the nation's countryside.

Many of Britain's most popular television shows are also filmed in Wales. Among them are the long-running science-fiction hit *Dr. Who* and its two spin-offs, *Torchwood* and *Class*. Another acclaimed Welsh-based show is the sitcom *Gavin and Stacey,* which was written by and stars Welsh actress Ruth Jones.

Wales has contributed many talented actors to the world of film and television. They include Richard Burton, Anthony Hopkins, Michael Sheen, and Catherine Zeta-Jones. The Welsh film industry is small, but it has produced several notable filmmakers, such as Justin Kerrigan and Sara Sugarman. Most Welsh films are made in English, but two Welsh-language films—*Hedd*

The cast and crew of *Dr. Who* prepare to film a scene on a beach in Wales. The show has been filming in Cardiff and the surrounding area since 2005.

Wyn and *Solomon a Gaenor*—have been nominated for the Academy Award for Best Foreign Language Movie.

Obsessed by Rugby

The Welsh are known for their love of sports—both watching them and playing them. But in Wales one sport stands above all others: Rugby is something of a national obsession. For many people, loving rugby is a defining feature of being Welsh.

A Rugby Star

When Welsh rugby fans argue over who is the greatest player ever, one name inevitably comes up—Gareth Edwards. In the 1960s and 1970s, when Wales's team dominated European rugby, Edwards was its best all-round player.

Born in 1947, Edwards grew up in the mining village of Gwaun-Cae-Gurwen in south Wales. In 1967, at nineteen, he played his first game on the Welsh national team. The next year, he became the youngest player to serve as the team's captain. Between 1967 and 1978, Edwards played fifty-three games for Wales and scored twenty tries—similar to touchdowns in American football.

Strong and agile, Edwards had a career full of game-changing moments. The most dramatic came in 1973, when Edwards was playing on a British invitational team known as the Barbarians. The Barbarians were pitted against the All Blacks from New Zealand. In a breathtaking play, Edwards carried the ball thirty yards before hurling himself over the touchline. Often merely referred to as "that try," Edwards's achievement has been called the greatest try in rugby history.

Since leaving the game, Edwards has found success in business and as a television sports commentator. In 1997, he became one of the first inductees in the International Rugby Hall of Fame.

Legend holds that rugby was invented at the Rugby School in England in 1823. It was a variation on soccer, called football in the United Kingdom. Like soccer, rugby is played by two teams that score points by moving a ball into a goal or goal line. Unlike in soccer, though, rugby players can carry as well as kick the ball. The ball in rugby is also oval-shaped rather than round.

Rugby teams in Wales now play two versions of the game—rugby union and rugby league. The play in rugby league is

Fans pack Millennium Stadium in Cardiff to watch the Welsh national rugby team play. Most people wear red shirts to match the team's jerseys.

usually faster and rougher than in rugby union. Rugby union is much more popular.

Wales's national rugby union team competes in the Six Nations Championship each year with teams from England, Scotland, Ireland, Spain, and Italy. The national team also vies for the Rugby World Cup, a competition between the best teams in the world. In 1999, Wales hosted the Rugby World Cup at the new Millennium Stadium in Cardiff. Now called the Principality Stadium, it is the largest sports arena in Wales.

A Sporting Nation

Almost rivaling the Welsh people's love of rugby is their enthusiasm for soccer. Wales has its own soccer league. The cities of Cardiff, Swansea, and Wrexham also have teams that play in the English soccer league. The national team of Wales participates in international soccer competitions as well.

Wales is very loyal to its rugby and soccer stars. Legendary athletes—such as rugby players Gareth Edwards and Neil Jenkins and soccer players John Charles and Gareth Bale—are often treated like national heroes. The Welsh are also proud of their Olympic athletes, who compete on the Great Britain team. At the Olympic Games in 2016, they won a record ten

More Welsh people play soccer than any other sport.

medals. Four Welsh athletes took home the gold: tae kwon do athlete Jade Jones, sailor Hannah Mills, and cyclists Elinor Barker and Owain Doull.

But as much as the Welsh like to root for their athletic stars, they love playing sports even more. Many people play soccer on local teams. Others like to hike, play golf, go horseback riding, and ride bicycles or motorbikes. People often visit Snowdonia National Park to go rock climbing and white-water rafting.

Jade Jones (in blue) won an Olympic gold medal in tae kwon do in 2012 and again in 2016.

A rock climber makes his way up a cliff in Snowdonia National Park.

Wales's long coastline also has plenty to offer amateur athletes. During the summer, its beaches are ideal for swimming and surfing. Many people also enjoy sailing and kayaking. To take full advantage of Wales's unspoiled coasts, Welsh athletes have even invented a new sport called coasteering. This physically demanding pastime combines swimming, rock climbing, and cliff jumping.

CHAPTER 10

The Welsh Way

DAILY LIFE IN WALES IS SIMILAR TO THAT IN OTHER modern English-speaking nations. Particularly in urban areas, people in Wales are likely to live in much the same way people do in the rest of the United Kingdom, Canada, or the United States.

But in Wales, some uniquely Welsh customs and behaviors remain alive. The most common is the use of the Welsh language. Although only about 19 percent of the population can speak Welsh, it remains the everyday language of many people living in the country.

Opposite: **Welsh teenagers leap into the sea on a hot summer day. Nearly a quarter of Welsh people are under the age of twenty.**

Rural Life

Most of the Welsh now live in cities. City dwellers tend to live fast-paced lives as they cope with new technologies and a changing economy. The ways of rural people, however, often stay the same from year to year. In many respects, their lives are little different from the Welsh living decades or even centuries earlier.

In rural areas, many people still work on farms. As they raise crops and tend herds of sheep and cattle, their routines are closely tied to changes in the landscape and the seasons.

A woman works in her garden outside her stone house.

Their houses are modest. Often people live in simple stone cottages built long ago. The daily lives of people in rural areas are centered on their community. They tend to have stronger ties to their families and their religion than city dwellers do.

Some Welsh people are afraid that the old rural way of life will soon be lost forever. In many communities, the population is rapidly aging, as young people leave to work in the cities. Shops, schools, and chapels—once the focus of people's social world—are closing as the number of residents shrinks.

Many farmers are also struggling to get by. A few are trying to revamp their farms to produce organic vegetables and meat to sell to specialty shops and restaurants. In addition, Welsh

Few people in Wales attend church on a regular basis. Some churches that are no longer needed have been converted into art galleries or inns.

Oranges and Lemons

For centuries, Welsh children have played oranges and lemons. The game's name sounds pleasant enough, but the song the players sing ends with some fairly gruesome lyrics:

> Here comes a candle to light you to bed.
> Here comes a chopper to chop off your head!
> Chip chop chip chop the last man's dead!

At the beginning of the game, two players decide one of them will be the leader of the orange team and the other the leader of the lemon team. They then face each other, holding their arms up and clasping hands to form a bridge.

While everyone sings, the other players run under the bridge one by one. When they all shout, "chop off your head!" the team leaders lower their arms, trapping one unlucky player. That player then chooses to be an orange or a lemon and stands behind the corresponding team leader, clasping his or her waist.

The game continues until all the players have been

caught and are lined up as part of the orange or lemon team. The two team leaders in front then clasp hands, and the teams play tug-of-war until one team falls down.

farmers are uncertain how the United Kingdom leaving the European Union will effect livelihoods.

The Foods of Wales

Today, the Welsh eat a wide range of foods available in grocery stores and restaurants. They also often enjoy traditional dishes the Welsh have been eating for centuries. Traditional Welsh cuisine usually features vegetables, lamb, and beef—foods commonly produced on Wales's farms. Because so much of

Wales lies near coastal waters, fish and shellfish are a large part of the native diet.

Welsh dishes tend to be hearty. In the past, they needed to be filling enough to keep a farmer or miner going strong all day. A typical traditional meal is cawl, a stew made of lamb, bacon, potatoes, and cabbage. Another favorite dish is Welsh rarebit, which combines toast with a cheese sauce.

Hearty Welsh meals usually include meat and potatoes.

Welsh Rarebit

One of Wales's most famous foods is Welsh rarebit. This dish combines melted cheese and toasted bread to create a tasty meal. Ask an adult to help you with this recipe.

Ingredients

8 ounces grated cheddar cheese

2 teaspoons flour

¼ teaspoon Dijon mustard

4 slices toasted bread

1 tablespoon butter

¼ cup milk

pinch of pepper

Directions

Use a fork or whisk to mix the cheese, butter, flour, milk, mustard, and pepper in a saucepan. Place the saucepan on a stovetop and turn the heat on low. Stir the cheese mixture until it melts into a thick sauce.

Place two pieces of toast on two plates. Top the toast with the warm cheese sauce and serve.

Laverbread is part of a traditional Welsh breakfast. Despite its name, laverbread is not really a bread. It is a paste made of boiled seaweed. Often laverbread is rolled in oatmeal and fried to make little cakes. It is typically served with bacon and cockles, a type of shellfish.

There are plenty of actual breads and cakes in traditional Welsh cooking. Welsh cakes are particularly popular. These small, sugary treats are flavored with dried fruit and cooked on a griddle. Another favorite is *bara brith*, a moist fruitcake made with tea.

In Welsh cities, a lively restaurant scene has recently emerged. Many showcase special versions of traditional Welsh fare. They also feature delicacies such as locally made cheeses and Welsh black beef. But for everyday dining, the Welsh are more likely to go to a pub. Pubs are bars that offer basic lunches and dinners. Meeting friends at a pub is a common social activity, especially in country villages.

Welsh cakes are sold at shops throughout the country. They are often eaten as a snack with tea.

Going to Festivals

The Welsh also love to socialize at the festivals and fairs held throughout the year. For more than three decades, the Hay Festival has brought artists and thinkers together at Hay-on-Wye, a town near Brecon Beacons National Park. Beyond the Border is an international storytelling festival held at St. Donat's Castle. Gladfest, hosted by Gladstone's Library in northeastern Wales, invites visitors to celebrate the written word by participating in creative writing workshops. A recent addition to Wales's festival schedule, Swn is a three-day festival in Cardiff celebrating new bands and musical acts.

The event most associated with Wales is the Eisteddfod—a festival of music, dance, and poetry. The first modern Eisteddfod was held in 1792. It was based on contests held in the Middle Ages, during which musicians and bards performed before Welsh princes.

Eisteddfodau (the plural of Eisteddfod) are now held all over Wales. Among the most notable is the Welsh League of Youth's annual Eisteddfod just for children. The small town of Llangollen in northeastern Wales also hosts the Llangollen International Musical Eisteddfod every summer. Meant to foster peace, the festival features amateur choirs from around the world.

The biggest, though, is the National Eisteddfod. It is held in August, with its location alternating between north and south Wales. Each year, about 150,000 people come together for this event to enjoy all sorts of music, from traditional choral singing to rock and roll. The National Eisteddfod also features the initiation of new members into the Gorsedd. This exclusive group of poets and musicians is charged with working to preserve the Welsh language.

Holidays in Wales

The Welsh have their own unique ways of celebrating many holidays. Some treasured traditions are no longer widely practiced, and others that had fallen out of use are being revived.

One beloved old Welsh Christmas tradition that is beginning to find a new foothold is the *plygain*. From 3:00 a.m. to 6:00 a.m. on Christmas Day, congregants gather in rural churches to listen to male choirs sing Christmas carols. The hours before the plygain are called Noson Gyflaith, or "Toffee Evening." Everyone stays awake by making and eating toffee candy, playing games, and telling stories.

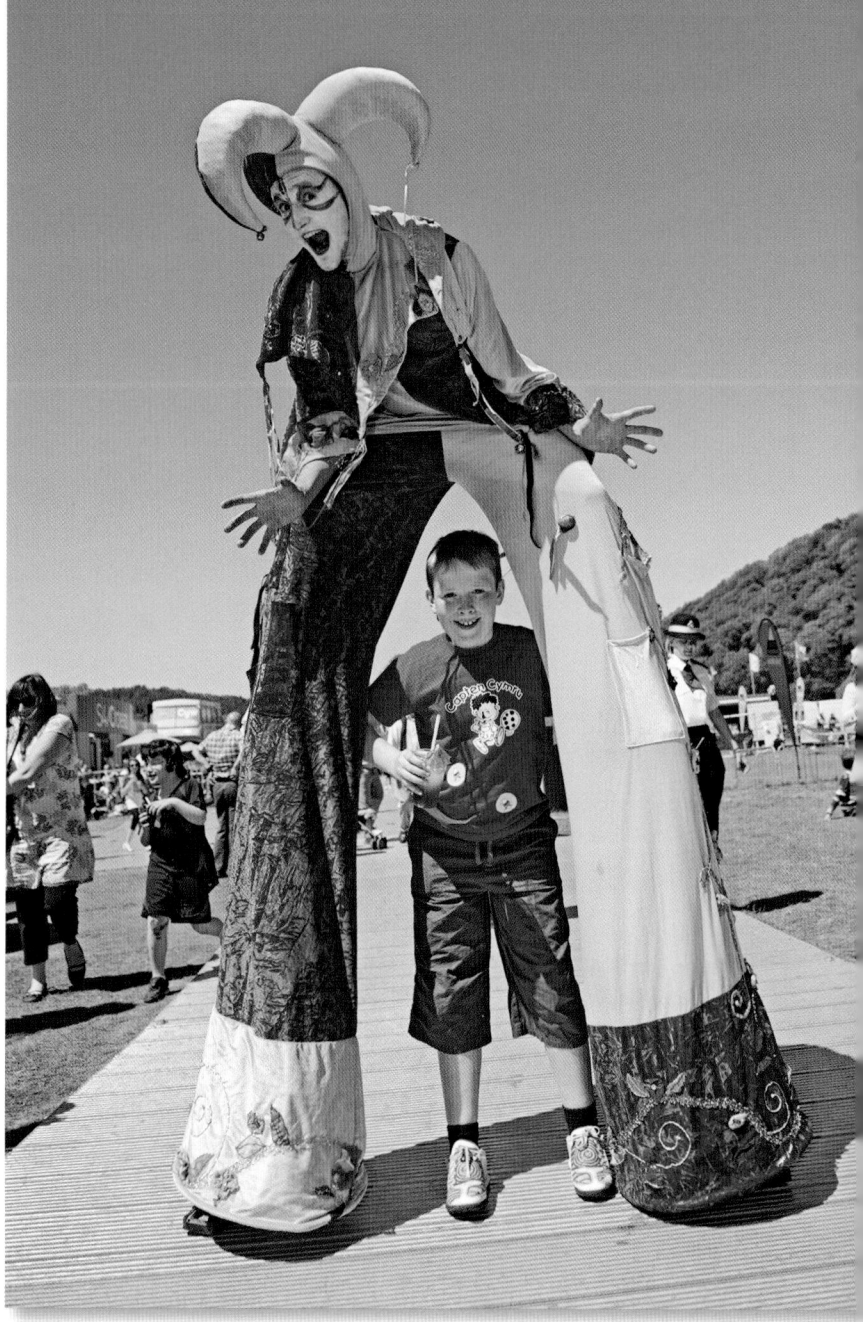

A stilt walker poses with a boy at an Eisteddfod festival.

In some parts of Wales, there is a tradition of people plunging into the sea on New Year's Day.

In some areas of Wales, Welsh children still celebrate New Year's Day with the tradition of *calennig*. They go door-to-door, giving friends and neighbors good wishes for the new year ahead. At each house, the children sing a song, and the family inside rewards them with a few coins.

The Welsh celebrate Valentine's Day on February 14, but they also have their own romantic holiday—St. Dwynwen's Day. In the fourth century, a girl named Dwynwen fell in love with a young man. Her father would not let her marry him, so she vowed never to wed. Dwynwen became a Catholic nun and founded a convent in northwest Wales.

Because of her wish that God help those in love, St.

Public Holidays

New Year's Day	January 1
Good Friday	March or April
Easter Monday	March or April
Early May bank holiday	First Monday in May
Spring bank holiday	Last Monday in May
Summer bank holiday	First Monday in August
Christmas	December 25
Boxing Day	December 26

Dwynwen is now considered the patron saint of lovers. Every January 25, her saint day, Welsh couples exchange gifts and go out for romantic dinners. Not everyone celebrates St. Dwynwen's Day, but it is becoming a more popular holiday every year, especially among Welsh speakers.

Celebrating All Things Welsh

Each year, Wales's grandest celebration happens on March 1. Called St. David's Day, the holiday commemorates Wales's

Welsh Love Spoons

Hundreds of years ago, if a Welsh man fell in love with a woman, he would pull out a pocketknife, find a block of wood, and begin carving. The result would be a love spoon—a traditional token of affection.

Love spoons were less utensils than works of art. Carved into their handles were symbols that represented promises. A heart assured a man's sweetheart that he would always love her. A key promised her security. And a wheel was a pledge that he would be a hard worker.

A skillfully made love spoon also sent a message to the beloved woman's family. It was an assurance that the carver would be a good provider. After all, a man who could carve such a spoon could probably earn a decent living as a woodworker.

Welsh craftspeople still make love spoons. People often purchase them as gifts for weddings, anniversaries, and birthdays.

patron saint. But, even more than that, it is a celebration of everything Welsh.

In cities, people parade down the streets, waving the Welsh dragon flag and black banners bearing a gold cross, the flag of St. David. They also go to concerts, street parties, and food festivals. Everyone indulges in Welsh cakes, bara brith, and the other delicacies their nation is known for.

Many students go to school for just a half day. To celebrate St. David's Day, classrooms suspend their regular lessons, and instead, students spend a few hours singing songs and reciting poems in a school Eisteddfod.

Children also celebrate the holiday by dressing up in costumes dating from the eighteenth century. Girls wear long petticoats and tall hats atop frilly bonnets. Boys don white shirts, black pants, and fitted black overcoats. Men and women often pin to their lapels a daffodil or a leek, two symbols of Wales.

The festivities provide the Welsh with a reminder of all the things they love about their land—the stirring landscapes, the proud history, the old songs and stories, and most of all the Cymry themselves—their fellow countrymen. On this day, everyone, English speakers and Welsh speakers alike, greet each other in their country's ancient language. "Dydd Gwyl Dewi Hapus!" they say, wishing one and all a "Happy St. David's Day."

A man dressed in an old-fashioned costume leads a St. David's Day parade in Cardiff.

Timeline

Wales becomes a leading producer of iron and coal during the Industrial Revolution.	late 1700s
Welsh protesters as part of the Chartist movement march on Newport and demand the right to vote.	1839
David Lloyd George becomes the first Welshman to be named prime minister of the United Kingdom.	1916
Plaid Cymru, a political party dedicated to Welsh independence, is founded.	1925
The Welsh Language Society is established to promote the use of Welsh.	1962
At the village of Aberfan, 144 people are killed in a landslide of industrial waste from a nearby coal mine.	1966
Welsh voters elect representatives to the first National Assembly for Wales.	1999
A referendum passes allowing the National Assembly to create laws for Wales without the approval of the British Parliament.	2011
Fifty-three percent of the Welsh choose to leave the European Union in the Brexit vote.	2016

1776	The U.S. Declaration of Independence is signed.
1789	The French Revolution begins.
1865	The American Civil War ends.
1879	The first practical lightbulb is invented.
1914	World War I begins.
1917	The Bolshevik Revolution brings communism to Russia.
1929	A worldwide economic depression begins.
1939	World War II begins.
1945	World War II ends.
1969	Humans land on the Moon.
1975	The Vietnam War ends.
1989	The Berlin Wall is torn down as communism crumbles in Eastern Europe.
1991	The Soviet Union breaks into separate states.
2001	Terrorists attack the World Trade Center in New York City and the Pentagon near Washington, D.C.
2004	A tsunami in the Indian Ocean destroys coastlines in Africa, India, and Southeast Asia.
2008	The United States elects its first African American president.
2016	Donald Trump is elected U.S. president.

Fast Facts

Official name: Wales

Capital: Cardiff

Official languages: Welsh, English

Cardiff

Welsh flag

Official religion:	None
Year of founding:	1536 (first Act of Union)
National anthem:	"God Save the Queen" (official), "Land of My Fathers" (unofficial)
Government:	Parliamentary constitutional monarchy (as part of the United Kingdom)
Head of state:	Monarch
Head of government:	Prime minister
Area:	8,015 square miles (20,759 sq km)
Latitude and longitude of geographic center:	52°19' N, 3°46' W
Bordering country:	England to the east
Highest elevation:	Mount Snowdon, 3,556 feet (1,084 m)
Lowest elevation:	Sea level along the coast
Average daily high temperature:	In Cardiff, 47°F (8°C) in January, 71°F (22°C) in July
Average daily low temperature:	In Cardiff, 36°F (2°C) in January, 56°F (13°C) in July
Average annual precipitation:	50 inches (127 cm)

Anglesey Island

Snowdonia National Park

National population (2016 est.): 3,113,200

Population of major cities (2015 est.):

Cardiff	345,810
Swansea	182,361
Newport	130,086
Wrexham	62,487
Merthyr Tydfil	44,265

Landmarks:
- ▶ *Conwy Castle,* Conwy
- ▶ *Dylan Thomas Centre,* Swansea
- ▶ *Snowdonia National Park*, Gwynedd
- ▶ *St. Fagans National Museum,* Cardiff
- ▶ *St. David's Cathedral*, Pembrokeshire

Economy: Until recently, coal mining was the most important industry in Wales. But with dropping coal prices, Wales worked to revamp its economy in the late twentieth century. The economy is now focused on the manufacturing and service industries, although a small number of people still continue to farm and raise livestock. Tourism has also become a leading source of revenue for Wales.

Currency: The British pound. In 2017, £1 equaled US$1.30, and US$1.00 equaled 77p.

Currency

System of weights and measures: Metric system

Literacy rate: 88% (English speakers), 63% (Welsh speakers)

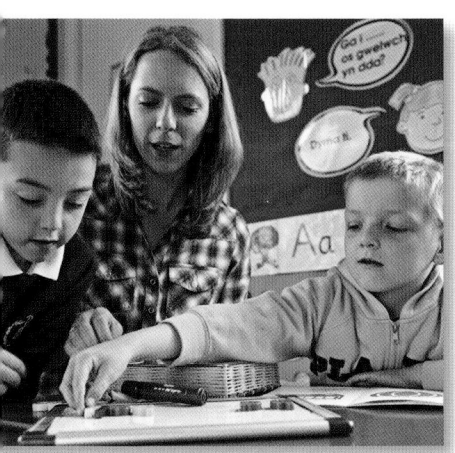

Schoolchildren

Common Welsh words and phrases:		
	Sut mae	Hello
	Hwyl fawr	Good-bye
	Bore da	Good morning
	Nos da	Good night
	Os gwelwch in dda	Please
	Diolch	Thank you
	Croeso	You're welcome
	Sut ydych chi?	How are you?
	Ie	Yes
	Nage	No

Prominent Welsh:		
	Shirley Bassey *Singer*	(1937–)
	John Charles *Soccer player*	(1931–2004)
	Gareth Edwards *Rugby player*	(1947–)
	David Lloyd George *Prime minister*	(1863–1945)
	Owain Glyndwr *Revolutionary leader*	(ca.1350–ca.1415)
	Carwyn Jones *First minister*	(1967–)
	Iolo Morganwg *Scholar and poet*	(1747–1826)
	Dylan Thomas *Poet*	(1914–1953)

Dylan Thomas

To Find Out More

Books

- Forrester, Kate. *Celtic Tales: Fairy Tales and Stories of Enchantment from Ireland, Scotland, Brittany, and Wales.* San Francisco: Chronicle, 2016.

- Thomas, Dylan. *A Child's Christmas in Wales.* New York: Holiday House, 2017.

- *Wales.* Oakland, CA: Lonely Planet Publications, 2017.

Videos

- *Extreme Wales with Richard Parks.* Bath, England: One Tribe TV, 2016.

- *The Story of Wales.* Directed by John Geraint, Sophie Elwin-Harris, and Jeff Morgan. Richmond Hill, Ontario: BFS Entertainment, 2012.

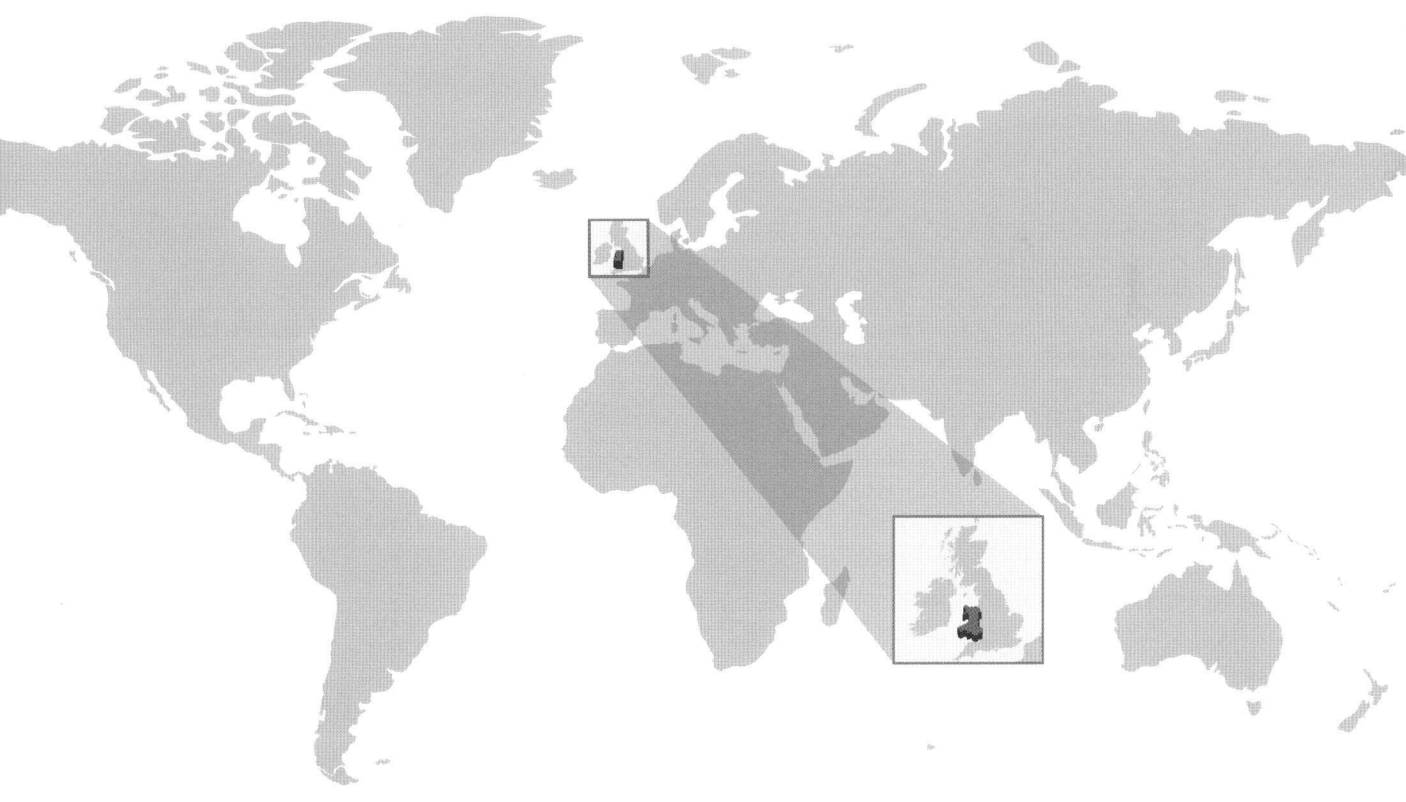

▶ Visit this Scholastic website for more information on Wales:
www.factsfornow.scholastic.com
Enter the keyword **Wales**

Index

Page numbers in *italics* indicate illustrations.

Meet the Author

LIZ SONNEBORN, A GRADUATE OF Swarthmore College in Pennsylvania, lives in Brooklyn, New York. She has written more than one hundred books for adults and young readers, specializing in American and world history and biography. Her books include *The Ancient Aztecs*, *The Mexican-American War*, *The American West*, and *A to Z of American Indian Women*. Sonneborn is also the author of numerous volumes for the Enchantment of the World Series, including *Mexico*, *North Korea*, *Pakistan*, *France*, and *Tibet*.

Photo Credits

Photographs ©:

cover: VisitBritain/Britain on View/Getty Images; back cover: Ric Ergenbright/Alamy Images; 2: Robert Birkby/AWL Images; 5: Cody Duncanage fotostock; 6 left: Billy Stock/Shutterstock; 6 center: The Photolibrary Wales/Alamy Images; 6 right: Tonybrindley/Dreamstime; 7 left: Vlue/Dreamstime; 7 right: FLPA/Wayne Hutchinson/age fotostock; 8: Lordprice Collection/Alamy Images; 11: phildaint/Shutterstock; 12: Funkystock/age fotostock; 13: Rebel and patriot Owen Glendower (gouache on paper), English School, (20th century)/Private Collection/© Look and Learn/Bridgeman Art Library; 14: Kathy deWitt/Alamy Images; 16: Billy Stock/Shutterstock; 19: Helen Hotson/Shutterstock; 20: robertharding/age fotostockage fotostock; 21: bob mazzer/Alamy Images; 22: Duncan Maxwell/age fotostock; 23 left: nicolamargaret/iStockphoto; 23 right: Matt Cardy/Getty Images; 24: The Photolibrary Wales/Alamy Images; 25: Sebastien Coell/Shutterstock; 26: Drew Buckley/Alamy Images; 28: Nature Photographers Ltd/Alamy Images; 29 top: LellsP/Alamy Images; 29 bottom: Ben Birchall/Press Association/AP Images; 30: DGDImages/Alamy Images; 31: Wouter Pattyn/Minden Pictures/Superstock, Inc.; 32: jax10289/iStockphoto; 33: Tonybrindley/Dreamstime; 34: FLPA/Andrew Parkinson/age fotostock; 35: Keith Morris/age fotostock; 36: keith morris/Alamy Images; 38: Werner Forman Archive/age fotostock; 39: Media Wales; 40: CM Dixon/age fotostock; 43: Museum of the City of New York/Mary Evans Picture Library; 45: World History Archive/Alamy Images; 46: Zoonar/Graham Mulroo/age fotostock; 47: Vlue/Dreamstime; 48: The National Library of Wales; 49: Morphart Creation/Shutterstock; 51: The Wentworth Collection/Mary Evans/age fotostock; 52: Jeff Morgan 15/Alamy Images; 53: Illustrated London News Ltd/Mary Evans/age fotostock; 56: Keystone-France/Gamma-Keystone/Getty Images; 57: PA Images/Alamy Images; 58: Matthew Horwood/Getty Images; 61: Bethany Clarke/Getty Images; 62: AP Images; 63: Matthew Horwood/Getty Images; 64: Aimee Herd/Alamy Images; 65: Edmund Sumner/VIEW/age fotostock; 66: Veronaa/Getty Images; 67: Dimitris Legakis/Rex Features/AP Images; 68 top: CW Images/Alamy Images; 70: FLPA/Wayne Hutchinson/age fotostock; 73: KBImages/Alamy Images; 75: Keith Morris/age fotostock; 76: OLI SCARFF/AFP/Getty Images; 77: elgol/iStockphoto; 78: Marilyn Barbone/Dreamstime; 81: D Legakis/Athena Picture Agency Ltd/Alamy Images; 82: Ian Dagnall/Alamy Images; 83: Richard Williams/Dreamstime; 85: Keith Morris/age fotostock; 86: wda bravo/Alamy Images; 88: Sherab/Alamy Images; 89: Paul Fearn/Alamy Images; 90: Steff Howells/Dreamstime; 92: keith morris/Alamy Images; 93: Kathy deWitt/Alamy Images; 94: ffoto_life/Alamy Images; 95: Geoff Abbott/Alamy Images; 96: Keith Morris/age fotostock; 98: nahariyani/Shutterstock; 99: eye35/Alamy Images; 100: Haydn Denman/Alamy Images; 101: Mark Baker/Sony Music Archive/Getty Images; 102: ARNOLDO MONDADORI EDITORE S.P./age fotostock; 103: Illustrated London News Ltd/Mary Evans/age fotostock; 104: Erich Auerbach/Popperfoto/Getty Images; 105: Everett Collection Inc./age fotostock; 106: Figure in a Village Street (oil on canvas), Williams, Kyffin (1918-2006) / Private Collection/Photo © Bonhams, London, UK/Bridgeman Art Library; 107: Cezza/Alamy Images; 108: Keith Morris/age fotostock; 109: Ed Lacey/Popperfoto/Getty Images; 110: FACUNDO ARRIZABALAGA/AFP/Getty Images; 111: keith morris/Alamy Images; 112: Wang Yuguo/Xinhua/Alamy Images; 113: David Pickford/age fotostock; 114: keith morris/Alamy Images; 116: Kathy deWitt/Alamy Images; 117: The Photolibrary Wales/Alamy Images; 118: Medici/Mary Evans/age fotostock; 119: walespix/Alamy Images; 120: Paul Cowan/Dreamstime; 121: foodanddrinkphotos/age fotostock; 123: Keith Morris/age fotostock; 124: CW Images/Alamy Images; 125: Photofusion/UIG/Getty Images; 126: Tom Williams/CQ Roll Call/AP Images; 127: Mark Hawkins/Barcroft Images/Barcroft Media/Getty Images; 130 left: CW Images/Alamy Images; 131 top: Veronaa/Getty Images; 131 bottom: Helen Hotson/Shutterstock; 132 bottom: elgol/iStockphoto; 132 top: Sebastien Coell/Shutterstock; 133 bottom: Erich Auerbach/Popperfoto/Getty Images; 133 top: Keith Morris/age fotostock.

Maps by Mapping Specialists.